ESSAYS ON RENEWAL

Essays on Renewal

Léon Joseph Suenens

SERVANT BOOKS
Ann Arbor, Michigan

"The World For Which the Lord Did Not Pray," translation by Rosemary Spitler © 1977 by Servant Publications. Published originally as "Le monde pour lequel le Seigneur n'a pas prie" in the April 20, 1975 issue of *La documentation catholique*, Paris.

"Commitment and Fidelity," translation reprinted courtesy of National Catholic News Service. Translated from a pastoral letter issued July, 14, 1971

"Christian Love and Human Sexuality" translation © 1976 by the Incorporated Catholic Truth Society, London. Reprinted with permission.

"The Church in the Face of Time" appeared as "L'eglise face au temps" in the Autumn 1970 issue of *The Ampleforth Journal* of Ampleforth Abbey, York, England.

"Charismatic Christians and 'Social' Christians," translated by Rosemary Spitler © 1977 by Servant Publications. Published originally as "Chrétiens charismatiques et chrétiens 'sociaux' " in the January 4, 1976 issue of *La documentation catholique*, Paris.

"What Can We do To Overcome Unnecessary Polarizations in the Church," reprinted from the October, 1973 issue of *Concilium*. Reprinted by permission of The Seabury Press.

"Who Is She?" translation by Rosemary Spitler © 1977 by Servant Publications. Published originally as "Quelle est celle-ci?" in the 1976 issue of *Magnificat*, Brussels.

"Where Do We go From Here?" reprinted courtesy of *The Listener*, London. Published originally in the July 25, 1974 issue of *The Listener*.

"The Council and Church Unity" reprinted courtesy of *Criterion*, Chicago. Published originally in the Spring, 1964 issue of *Criterion*.

"Toward Tomorrow's Church" reprinted courtesy of America Press. Originally published in the June, 1972, issue of *Catholic Mind*.

Published by Servant Books
P.O. Box 8617
Ann Arbor, Michigan 48017

Available from Servant Books
Distribution Center
237 N. Michigan
South Bend, Indiana 46601

ISBN 0-89283-047-6

Printed in the United States of America

CONTENTS

I
THE CHRISTIAN AND THE WORLD

II
THE CHRISTIAN

Introduction

On September 4, 1927, Leon Joseph Suenens was ordained a priest in Malines, Belgium by Cardinal Ernst Joseph van Roey. Thirty-four years later, Fr. Suenens succeeded Cardinal van Roey as Primate of Belgium, and in the years since he has emerged as one of the leading figures in the Catholic Church. Today, Cardinal Suenens is recognized throughout the world as one of the most thoughtful, visible, and vigorous of all Christian leaders.

We have collected and published these essays to commemorate the fiftieth anniversary of Cardinal Suenens's ordination to the priesthood. Cardinal Suenens has been pondering and analyzing the condition of the Church throughout his adult life, almost since his days as a seminarian in Rome in the mid-1920's. However, this collection is made up of essays written during the last decade. Taken as a whole, they portray the movement of renewal in the Church in the years following Vatican II. It is something of a shock to realize that of all the leading figures at Vatican II only Cardinal Suenens and Pople Paul VI are still alive. The Cardinal is thus a link with the recent as well as the more distant past, a link we hope is evident in these essays.

One is tempted to seek unifying themes in a career as varied as Cardinal Suenens's. Indeed, reflecting on the outlines of his life, it is difficult to imagine a more diverse pastoral ministry. Following his education in Rome, Fr. Suenens was in succession a seminary teacher, army chaplain, and Rector of the University of

Louvain. He was named auxiliary bishop of Malines in 1945, and soon displayed a talent for administration. Throughout the 1940s and 50s he coupled his episcopal duties with involvement in the rethinking of pastoral practices and strategies that was taking place in the nascent Cursillo Movement, Legion of Mary, and in other European renewal movements.

This quiet, effective work took on a different character after Bishop Suenens's friend, Pope John XXIII, named him to succeed Cardinal van Roey in 1961. Almost immediately, Cardinal Suenens emerged as one of the leaders of the Second Vatican Council. In the years since he has been a leader in implementing the changes dictated by the Council. Roman Catholics know him as a persuasive advocate of institutional changes in the Church. Christians of all denominations know him as a committed ecumenist and a leader of worldwide Christian renewal. Non-Christian men and women know him as one who speaks honestly and intelligibly about the gospel of Jesus Christ.

Cardinal Suenens's zealous devotion to the gospel is one theme that does unify his career. As a scholar, teacher, pastor, administrator, diplomat, ecumenist, public figure, and advocate of renewal, he has concerned himself with preaching the gospel to a world that is adrift because it has rejected its savior. "The world is dying because it does not know Jesus Christ," he told an ecumenical conference on the charismatic renewal in Kansas City this summer. It was a moving moment — an eminent Catholic prelate reminding a gathering of Protestants, Catholics, and Messianic Jews of the task before them, of the purpose of all their efforts to bring about Christian renewal.

This devotion to the gospel has motivated Cardinal Suenens's priesthood from the very beginning. Not long ago, he recalled the feeling that attracted him to the priesthood. He was a young boy, and the particular experience, he said, was one of great joy at the thought of eternity with God. "I felt the call to become a priest," he recalled, "with the idea that the best way to obtain a wonderful eternal life was to prepare many others for that life to come, for that everlasting life, by bringing to them the gospel as the way to eternity."

Honor is a suspect concept in our modern world. We return to an older and more humane tradition here as we honor Cardinal Suenens. All of us would do well to emulate this leader of God's people. All of us can honestly admire him. For fifty years he has served God and his Church unceasingly, with a joy, an enthusiasm, and a love that anticipates the eternity with God that awaits us all.

The Editors
Servant Books

The Christian and the World

The World for Which
The Lord Did Not Pray

When a true statement has been repeated untiringly for ten years, the truth of it finally becomes distorted as a result of unilateralism. Remember that each decade marks its own reaction against the gaps and deficiencies of the preceding era. Therefore, it is periodically necessary to reestablish a balance between complementary truths. The game of ebb and flow is not played only by the sea. As I write this, I am thinking of a declaration which today has become trite due to stating and restating it, namely, that the Christian must be *in* the world, open to its problems and ready to serve mankind. We have known a time when, in the face of excessive pessimism, it was necessary to demonstrate the positive values of the world and to encourage confidence in them. But owing to repetition, today it is urgent that we underline a fact: a Christian must not only be present to men, right in the heart of man's concerns and problems, but he must also eventually know how to take his part against the world, against a certain world for which Jesus did not pray.

We are familiar with Jesus' words at the Last Supper:

> I am praying for them; I am not praying for the world . . . I have given them Thy word; and the world

has hated them because they are not of the world,
even as I am not of the world.

(John 17:9,14)

A separation

The argument against that world also belongs to the
gospel. "This attitude toward the world," remarks the
exegete Raymond Brown in his magnificent commentary on St. John, "seems strange and scandalous to many
contemporary Christians, as if Jesus were only vaguely
familiar with the work of the apostolate and the task of
being present to the world." There is an opposition, a
contradiction, a separation which plays an integral part
in Christianity. Jesus did not hide from his followers the
fact that they would be contradictory signs, like himself
even, but he promised them an interior peace stronger
than the unavoidable hostility that awaits them. Jesus
never said we must not have enemies; he simply said we
must love them. That's quite different, and not quite so
easy!

During the Second Vatican Council, at the time of the
debate over the Constitution entitled *Gaudium et Spes*,
several bishops reacted against the excessive unilateral
optimism regarding the world reflected in the first
draft. Important corrections were brought up, propos-
ing to give a realistic image of the world; it was at once
an invitation, and to a real opening and to critical judgment. These reactions intended to underline the existence of a world that is subject to the forces of evil,
subject to obscure powers that menace the heart of man,
the heart of society.

A compromised peace?

It was not without reason that Jesus taught his disciples to say: "Lead us not into temptation, but deliver us
from evil." The temptation of Christians today is to accept a compromised peace with the world, to accept the

2

criteria of judgment and the basis for values from the surrounding milieu which conditions them. One cannot breathe polluted air without polluting his lungs. I am thinking particularly of ethical problems, the order of the day in our public discussions, which range from artificial insemination to euthanasia, and which pass through a whole gamut of moral problems present from birth to death: contraception, extramarital relations, abortion on demand, etc.

With respect to all these crucial problems, Christians enter into dialogue with non-Christians. There is a huge temptation to accept postulates that are foreign to our faith. It is not unlikely in a discussion of this type that the Christian will attempt to use arguments to convince his opponent, striving to reach him on the same wavelength. We have attempted, in the collective letter of the Belgian Episcopate concerning abortion, to say why respect for human life at its beginning is imperative for every man and every society, lest our very foundation should crumble. We appealed to reasons which do not imply a religious influence. But the Christian has other reasons which are valid for him: for the Christian, there is no natural order, properly speaking, on which is imposed a supernatural order. There is, in fact, only one order, founded in God, an order whose supreme reference is found in the mystery of the divine call of a man in response to the personal love of God. This unique order encompasses and implies nature, but it surpasses and sometimes contradicts nature, insofar as man, in his flesh and bone, is at odds with sin in all its forms: original sin, collective sin, personal sin.

A friend of mine who is a non-believer was telling me the other day that in politics he labels people "leftist" or "rightist" according to whether they believe in original sin. He was not referring to Christian dogma, but rather to an experienced reality, perceived in his daily circumstances, a reality which prescribes options of political wisdom, taking into account man such as he is, not his idealized image.

So my friend has joined with Pascal who wrote: "Without the mystery of original sin, the most incomprehensible of all, we are incomprehensible to ourselves . . . man is more inconceivable without this mystery, than is this mystery inconceivable to man" (Pensees de Pascal 434).

Legality and morality

It is necessary to order one's conscience not according to games of parliamentary majorities, as if a vote of 51 voices against 49 could determine good and evil in any given society, as if legality could be identified with morality. The law of numbers is not the law of morality— neither of private nor of public morality. The law of morality is not judged according to present-day practices or even legalized practices. If tomorrow some Parliament should find a majority in favor of bigamy, this would then become legal, but the law would remain in flagrant contradiction with moral and social good.

This realistic view of the world helps us to keep our distance where necessary. We can better understand how human laws subject to fluctuating public opinion are not the final criterion of morality.

In order to maintain their own identity, Christians will have to make heavy sacrifices, and dark clouds are gathering for them in a variety of countries. It is vital that each and every one of us be ready for options which good conscience will impose on us out of faithfulness to the gospel. Social conformity, the assumptions of a profit-oriented and consumer-oriented society as well as moral discussions in the heart of an increasingly permissive society—all that belongs to this world "for which the Lord did not pray."

An English author, Rosemary Haughton, by way of a

warning to Christians tempted by conformity, has written these striking lines:

> Perhaps we shall have to stop being good citizens, if the city belongs to the Prince of this world. We may have to stop being respectable and approved. It hasn't happened for a long time. It could be happening now, and we need to be aware of this change, because if we aren't then we may wake up one day and find we aren't Christians anymore, but only good, respectable citizens.

Commitment and Fidelity

Among the many reexaminations of the present time, people are challenging the very idea of a lasting fidelity within a life commitment. How can one irrevocably commit the future, they say, by a past decision, while we live in a moving, unforeseeable world? Can one fix forever a choice so conditioned and hazardous? If, as time goes on, such a life choice turns out to be an obstacle in the way of my personal fulfillment, why should it forever determine my life?

These questions come up again in relation to priestly or religious vocations: the young hesitate in the face of a definitive life orientation. These questions are at the heart of our discussions of fidelity when analyzing priestly or religious disengagements, so numerous today throughout the world and as painful for those involved as they are for the whole Christian community. These questions also feed the debate on conjugal fidelity and the extension of divorce.

All these problems are not identical and they must not be confused, but they have a common denominator: the questioning of fidelity. Just yesterday, fidelity went unquestioned. It was not always put into practice, but it was recognized as the basis of our way of life.

What is new is not that fidelity is being attacked. Gide

and others did that, but they proclaimed themselves "immoralists." Today people claim to be acting in the name of morality in liberating themselves from the constraints of fidelity, presented as a hindrance to their successive authenticities.

Fidelity to oneself

By a stange paradox, fidelity is challenged first of all in the name of fidelity to oneself.

Does not a man, it is asked, have the right and the duty to promote his own fulfillment? In case of conflict, doesn't fidelity to oneself take precedence over fidelity to another?

The opposition rests, it seems to me, on the ambiguity of the term: "fidelity to oneself." What can this expression mean in such a context? It is forgotten that, strictly speaking, fidelity, like justice, supposes otherness.

One is not just or unjust toward oneself, but with regard to another. One is not, in the strict sense, faithful to oneself, to the word pledged by oneself. It would be better to speak to the obligation we have of being constant, persevering, logical, and coherent with ourselves and with our previous resolutions or promises.

In the brochure "To live committed" published by the National Vocation Center, this necessary "distance" has opportunely been stressed. "No doubt," the authors write, "one may wonder whether one can be faithful to oneself. Authenticity, rather than fidelity, is that virtue 'of internal usage,' which consists in revealing oneself completely in one's truth. There is no doubt that there exists a certain 'fidelity' to the image one has of oneself. But as for commitment, one may wonder whether there exist relations with oneself that do not first of all pass by way of others. The image of self that I cherish in solitude is probably the one that I fashion from the expectations that others show in my regard. Fidelity in the full sense of the word is thought of and experienced in relation to a 'neighbor' who welcomes and stimulates the gift I give him: whether I call him God or the other, his mediation is necessary if I am to develop truly the commitment I have made. Thus is not fidelity to a cause or a task in reality fidelity to 'someone?' "

The notion of fidelity implies faith in others: the remark is important. The problem of fidelity has already been falsified if one begins by reducing it to fidelity to self and to the word given, once and for all, in the past.

In particular, opponents of the indissolubility of the marriage bond use as arguments those hastily contracted marriages, broken up for futile reasons and given such wide publicity in the press. But these were unions undertaken on a purely legal basis, without real mutual commitment of life and true love. So the conclusion could be that there had been no authentic marriage from the start, and that it is not a question of breaking up a marriage bond but rather of its nonexistence.

It is also evident that a "declared" commitment is valued by the content it deals with. In reality, in the true commitment, it is not a matter of committing oneself and then being faithful; fidelity is at the very heart of the profound commitment. Here there is no question of pure legal formality.

The lived experience of Christians who commit themselves in marriage, the priesthood, or the religious life is quite different. Commitment is not for them a verbal promise, a word given, but an act creating a certain type of intersubjective relation with the other and especially with God. They want this relation and live it as creative of their own personality, since on the level of being, man is defined essentially by relations consciously and freely assumed.

This commitment, and the fidelity that constantly re-creates this commitment, is situated in the depth of being. They are our sole true victory over the passage of time, our opening on the definitive, the eschatological, the eternal. To misunderstand that is to "reflatten" man to the biological and psychological level by stripping him of his spiritual and divine dimension. Commitment is exactly what makes me change level. It inaugurates a style of life in which I no longer allow myself to be torn apart by the fluctuations of instinct or emotion, nor carried away by every wind of doctrine. It is a style of life rooted in eternity (which the gospel tells us the believer experiences already) and founded on the certitude of love of the Other or of another. Here, I polarize in a new way my way of living. Fidelity is not at all a continuity productive of security, reassurance, routine, or fixity. It is a daily deepening of the ontological relation, a creation in order to respond to variable circumstances, a victory over temptations, a way of growing in trials. It alone renews a being's youth.

A freedom situated in time

In the last analysis, what underlies this discussion of fidelity is the very concept of man, the meaning of his life, and the significance of human freedom in his way of living.

True liberty implies the power received from God of freely determining our response to our vocation as sons of God for time and for eternity. This, the gospel warns us, will demand renunciation and abnegation, will often require that "the grain of wheat die." The dimension of eternity underlies the appeals of the Lord on behalf of fidelity, "Let man not separate what God has united;" and again, "He who, having once put his hand to the plow, looks back, is not worthy of the Kingdom."

That does not mean that there may not be errors in choices and options, and everything must be done to avoid them. When errors are made, if the subject cannot morally assume a truly human "commitment," it is legitimate that he not be forced to live a relation that he has not really willed and whose consequences he cannot accept. But these instances must not be multiplied through an erroneous concept of commitment and true human freedom.

Authentic freedom is situated in a history. It is proper to man to give meaning and continuity to his life: people too easily oppose a present choice to a decision taken previously.

Each present option is made in reference to a past on which each person depends; man lives his own history which makes one body with him. His freedom consists in the capacity to realize his plan throughout his life. He can construct his future and his life only to the extent to which his fundamental options of today keep their value for tomorrow. "To live," wrote Saint-Exupery, "is to be born slowly."

No doubt there may be certain life commitments that are taken through fear and distrust of self, to prohibit any going back, to drive oneself to future fidelity by burning one's boats. Such commitments have to be carefully examined. But the contrary is true also: it is because one is so sure that the choice will remain valid tomorrow that one commits one's self by a definitive decision.

At any rate, it remains true that each commitment must always be renewed to live and renourish its resolution of permanence. Speaking of the fidelity between spouses, Zundel defined it admirably in these words: "It is an ever-freer choice of an ever-stronger love."

It remains true that if certain values can lose their significance along the way, there are some that cannot by reason of their inherent virtue and quality, for they do not depend on personal fluctuations. Subjectivity is one thing; subjectivism is another.

There is a nobility proper to commitment that saves life from dissipation and confers on it vigor and strength.

There is pride too in lived continuity. "The joy of a man," Roger Garaudy stated recently at Assisi, "is to have remained faithful at 60 to the dream of his 20's." This statement recalls that of Alfred de Vigny: "Life is a dream of youth realized in maturity."

Fidelity to the other

Once the ambiguity of the expression "fidelity to oneself" has been set aside, what fidelity to others amounts to must be examined closely, whether that other be directly God in the priestly and religious commitment, or the spouse in the conjugal commitment. The living reference that determines fidelity is important for understanding fidelity from within and avoiding undue transpositions. But our purpose is not to compare these fidelities; it will suffice to sketch here some common traits.

Conjugal commitment is the mutual commitment of two persons who want to be united in view of a true community of life.

The magnificent formula of the English Ritual is well known:

> I take you for my lawful wife,
> to keep you from this day forward,
> for better or worse,
> in riches and in poverty.
> sickness and health,
> to love you and cherish you,
> till death do us part,
> in conformity with the holy will of God,
> and that is why I swear fidelity to you.

Marriage is a total commitment of two persons,

oriented toward one same plan: to build a community that is faithful and creative because it is founded on love.

For the Christian this human reality is raised to the level of a sacrament: a sign and expression of salvation in Jesus Christ. This union is prepared for and lived within a larger community: civil society, and, for the believer, the Church. The social dimension of marriage appears more and more as an essential constitutive element of the conjugal commitment.

Contemporary reflection on marriage brings to the foreground the notion of faithful commitment and the social dimension of the conjugal institution.

Human existence is not composed of solitary moments to be lived intensely until they run out. Quite the contrary, life is the continual decision to live each present as the outcome of a "before" and the preparation for an "after." By the plan that he assumes in committing himself, the individual decides to use his past to orient his future in a certain direction.

Fidelity—the fruit and condition of human commitment—is indissolubly creation and continuity: it implies the attentive consideration of directions chosen in the past and which make the present fruitful.

No doubt fidelity also implies the will to live "today" intensely and totally; but what would a "total" gift represent that would exclude these two essential dimensions of the person—his past and his future. If present fidelity wants to be radical, it must necessarily integrate the future of the one who seeks to live it.

A personal commitment is always situated within a human community. Besides expressing generally the conjunction of several wills directed toward the same objective, personal commitment is developed and created within a society which, in return, it seeks to enrich. Commitment wants to be a donation to others: it is the foundation of indispensable institutionalization.

A human person knows what he owes to the community that has borne him and which continues to nourish him. He is conscious, moreover, that he must enter a relation of exchange and bring to the society the creativity of which he is capable. It is a fundamental element of the stabilization and maturation of a person to be able to collaborate in the development of the community. The "personal good" is necessarily conditioned by the "common good" from which one profits and that one seeks to enrich. No doubt there are critical moments when the demands of the person seem incompatible with those of the community. If it is true that the community is directed to the promotion of the greatest number, no individual can assert the primacy of his own development over that of the collective. By the coercion that it exerts on its members, society seeks to encourage the coexistence and progress of the whole: it is normal that it can require of some the sacrifice of some prerogative or some right.

It is evident that the common good has often been used as a pretext for the oppression of the individual. It suffices to reread Diderot's "The Nun" to see how oppressive the power of certain parents or of society could be. But doesn't the law of human progress and even sometimes of simple duty demand personal renunciations? There are many professions, the medical for example, whose members are often called upon to sacrifice themselves for the welfare of others. Stressing the right of the person to his own fulfillment without regard to the social context risks falling into the snare of Marcuse, the philosopher of contestation. For him, mankind has always been ruled by two principles—that of pleasure and that of realism. As far as possible, all men have sought the maximum pleasure. But, since men have to live, to earn their salaries, to have themselves accepted by parents and by society, "realism" obliges them often to forego the agreeable. Marcuse affirms that in an un-threatened society of abundance, one can adopt the principle of pleasure alone. Is such a philosophy so different from the theory that would make the individual his law and goal without concerning himself either with others or with the common good? Such self-centeredness is a form of disguised narcissism and the negation of all commitment.

The genesis of a human commitment is a long and laborious work. But there comes a moment when the person wishes his commitment to take on a public form and assume social consequences. The "institutional moment," let us repeat, is determinative. It is the clear admission that a private commitment wants to be borne by the community and directed toward it. In this sense, the institutional moment is more than the official recognition of a reality already duly established. It gives an explicit social meaning to the commitment and in so doing modifies its impact profoundly. The given word is then lived both as an admission of one's personal plan and as a request to the community to accept it, to sustain it, and eventually to protect it.

At the institutional moment, the couple publicly proclaim that their commitment is no longer a purely private concern. They show awareness of being dedicated, thanks to the community which has raised them, to a work in which society participates and from which it profits: the building up of a radiant and creative home.

Far from enclosing love in a system of arbitrary constraints, the institutional moment seeks to expand that love to the dimensions of the larger collectivity. The emotional relationship certainly does not begin with the public exchange of consent; but it acquires all its meaning only when it involves the community itself of which each one is coresponsible.

Fidelity of God and to God

We believe that the concept of fidelity and commitment that these pages describe is valid for every man, believer or not. But, it must be admitted, it receives singular support and strength from faith in God.

A Christian can never forget that his fidelity is borne, sustained, vivified by the fidelity of God. The divine fidelity is at the heart of ours: it is its foremost support. Through him and in him the spouses love each other, not with a human love alone, personal and fragile, but with the very love of God. The sacrament of marriage penetrates with its grace the heart of the man and woman to raise them beyond themselves and to eternalize in them and with them the love that brought them together.

When it is a matter of fidelity and commitment in a priestly or religious vocation, this reference to God is still more visible and appears in the foreground.

I have heard the duty of fidelity to God in religious commitment challenged on the pretext that God is invisible, distant, unattainable by our concepts and by our language and that, therefore, all must be in reference to man and his needs.

It would distort the very meaning of alliance to suppress one of its terms. Such agnosticism is not only incompatible with faith; it falsifies the very data of the problem, by truncating the terms of the equation. The "I know in whom I have believed" is the soul of every priestly and religious vocation.

For the Christian, clergy and laity, God is the Real, the Living, the Present par excellence. He is, said St. Augustine, more "I than I myself."

Faith is a welcome and a meeting, it makes us realize and live the words of Claudel, on the eve of his conversion: "God: you have suddenly become someone." And

15

this "someone" is such that he becomes the unique *raison-d'etre* of our life.

This vision of faith does not eliminate the difficulties of the road, but it helps powerfully to confront them, to put them in place, to overcome them. The fidelity of God is at the basis of the requirement of a stable response—through and beyond time—on the part of man. It helps us to anticipate already here below that "Kingdom of God"—to come and already present—in which the wear and tear of time and the weakness of men will no longer prevail because the love that is God himself will triumph in the heart of every human love forever established in fidelity.

Christian Love and Human Sexuality

Introduction

In a recent declaration of the Sacred Congregation for the Doctrine of Faith on "Certain Questions Concerning Sexual Ethics" bishops were invited to "elucidate" for the faithful the teaching of Christianity concerning sexual morality. It would entail enlightening the consciences of those confronted with new situations, studying traditional teaching more deeply, and enriching it with a discernment of all the factors that can truthfully and profitably be brought forward as to the meaning and value of human sexuality.*

I would like to reply to this invitation by reflecting on a theme that is intimately bound to those choices which, though often unformulated or implicit, determine nevertheless the attitude of each individual to life, love, and freedom.

There are, it is true, other spheres in which the future of mankind is being determined, involving moreover the "power of love" which ought to be its motivating force: peace among nations, the safeguarding of freedom,

---

*Persona humana, paragraph 13. Future citations from this document are given by page number.

17

economic justice, respect for life. These are vital preoccupations that the thinking Christian cannot afford to neglect. However, taking as my point of reference the Roman document, I shall limit myself here to a two-fold purpose. On the one hand, I shall try to say what Christian love ought to be if it is to respond today both to the human vocation and to the demands of the gospel. On the other hand, I shall suggest a few specific ways of putting into practice this ideal in the matter of sexuality.

The "problem of morality"

Admittedly dialogue is by no means easy between those whose task it is to recall basic principles and those who would have it that morality is built on life itself. (Matt. 28:19; 2 Tim. 4:2). The latter, without going so far as to reduce morality to mere conformity with the *mores* predominant at a given time, maintain that experience is a major factor in clarifying and giving precision to moral laws.

While this attention to concrete facts has of course to be recognized, facts cannot, however, dictate laws. It is readily affirmed that first-hand experience is the basis of morality. But what are we to think of this affirmation? Definition gives rise to ambiguity: it should imply that moral norms only ratify contemporary *mores*. And what justification is there for assuming a conformity such as this?

It is true, however, that the "problem of morality" can present itself really only in the face of concrete choices. It is in the presence of obstacles or particular choices that we are aware of the need of a "compass" and directions to follow.

If many today take issue with inhuman situations in our consumer society, it is because such "realities of life" are in opposition to principles of justice and solidarity. What can be said is that the moral life, in so far as experience is concerned, contains within itself a "stance" of conscience which somehow precedes theoretical reflection. Morality, as the science of norms, must take into account what a well-informed moral sense offers in terms of specific judgments.

Likewise we hear repeatedly: "We do not need moral directives. It is for each to follow his own conscience." The truth in this statement lies in the fact that moral behavior is always the behavior of a particular person in a specific situation. Hence the indispensable role of the individual conscience.

But we must also stress that the conscience in making a particular decision has to take into account the objective meaning of the situation with which it is confronted. And this presupposes that the conscience is informed. For the Christian this implies the need of a continuous formation, beginning in early education and prolonged through one's entire life, in the light of the Scriptures, the Word of God, and of the Magisterium of the Church, the authoritative interpreter of our moral tradition.

Christian norms

At the very outset, then, it must be said that the Christian life should not be envisaged first and foremost as obedience to an assemblage of rules laid down by God to govern our behavior. The center of gravity in a moral judgment cannot be reduced to mere categories of what is "permitted" and what is "forbidden." The heart of morality is the basic choice which gives meaning to our life and, normally, inspires individual decisions.

The morality of a Christian is to be judged primarily according to whether he directs his life toward Jesus Christ and his message or whether he turns away from him. This does not mean at all that particular acts are unimportant. But this importance is secondary—the acts being only the "epiphany," the "manifestation," of the basic intention which inspires them.

Essentially, Christian morality is first and foremost a "covenant morality" to which the Christian is invited to respond in faith, hope, and love. It is in God that human love has its source and it is from him that it derives its vitality. It is within him that the total development of the human person is rooted. Within this perspective a moral norm is not primarily a restriction or a prohibition. It is in the nature of a signpost or a map or a fence which prevents a disastrous fall.

Against this background of "covenant morality," we must not confine moral choice to the alternative "sinful" or "not sinful." Morality is a call to advance in the direction of what is good—ultimately, that is, in the direction of God. "What we look for from the Church," it has been said, "is an incentive to go forward." This was put well by Msgr. Etchegaray, currently president of the Conference of the Bishops of France:

> Christian morality is simply the morality of the Creed: Christianity is neither faith without law nor law without faith. We must avoid toppling into pure subjectivity, the plague of our times. The gospel call has an objective content, but cannot, on that account, be reduced to a mere "moral system" ... Morality means living to the very best of oneself: choosing the fulfillment of one's potential.*

Love and Sexuality

Within this positive and constructive perspective I would like to invite every Christian to take note of the demands made by Christianity in the delicate sphere of

*La Croix, 30 March 1976, p. 8.

sexual* behavior. And to begin with, I think it imperative to clarify the meaning of the word "love" and point out ambiguities in current usage.

The word "love" is one of the most commonly used in our vocabulary today. It comes to us on the radio, on television, in countless songs, in films, and in literature. We meet it everywhere. Unhappily there are hidden beneath this wonderful word what can only be called counterfeits of love. Actually, the word is often used to glamorize the sexual instinct and its sovereign freedom.

A Chinese sage, asked one day what he would do if he were lord of the world, replied: "I would restore the meaning of words." An immense service indeed to mankind! In this matter Christians have a special responsibility not to allow the word "love" to be profaned. They should restore its meaning and use it only to express authentic love. It is imperative to keep love and sexuality in their proper places and not confuse them.

We cannot go into details here. It is enough to recall some of the differences between love and the sexual drive.

In my book *Love and Control* some years ago, I stressed certain points of contrast.

"Of course," I wrote, "we cannot dissociate the sexual instinct and love to the point of locating the first in man's animal nature, the second in his spiritual. This would be to forget that man is a unity: that even his animal nature is charged with a spirituality proper to him as a human being. But it remains true that the sexual instinct, even if

---

*The words "sexual" and "genital" are not synonymous. Sex and sexuality qualify our very being. The genital expression of sexuality is only one form of expression and is not to be identified with sexuality as such. However, unless the context indicates otherwise, terms such as "sexual instinct" and "sexual pleasure" used in these pages will generally imply a genital expression of sexuality.

it involves a certain degree of sharing—a kind of communion—is still directed toward the possession and subjugation of the partner.

"Love, on the contrary, is based on respect for the other: respect is as necessary for love as is air for the lungs. 'I could not love you as I do,' a poet wrote to his wife, 'if I did not revere you still more.'

"Love is never the egoism of two persons nor is it a search for self by means of the other. Love is giving; it does not seek to possess. To reduce love simply to a search for sexual pleasure is to atrophy love. It is not in the name of her doctrine and all that this entails, but in the name of love that the Church lays down as the first norm of love that it be true to itself, that it respect its own essential nature. What the Church criticizes in contemporary literature is not that it glorifies love, but that it does not know what real love is, that it does not even cross the threshold of love's kingdom, remaining pitiably remote from the nobility of what is genuinely human.

"Love and pleasure derived from sex are distinct to the degree that sometimes the two are entirely separate. At the lowest level, there is this kind of separation in debauchery. Prostitution, which is diametrically opposite to love, shows that physical satisfaction is one thing, love another.

"In a report on the role of men in prostitution, Dr. René Biot wrote quite rightly: 'The whole problem is to determine whether sexuality in man is the same force as that which drives animals to mate or if it is stamped by a spiritual component which radically alters its nature. If the first hypothesis is true, there is no reason why a man should not find a partner just anywhere, on the streets or in brothels. If, however, as we wholeheartedly believe, human sexuality is necessarily part of a much more complex unity, if human nature itself requires that sexuality be 'spiritually transformed into love,' then a sexual act performed by a man outside the exclusive, definitive love consecrated in marriage is not only a weakness which diminishes his moral dignity—it is a caricature of full human sexuality. The intrinsic evil of prostitution is that it causes man to lose sight of the fact that his sexual powers should never be dissociated from love. Let us not speak merely of attraction, for this can remain only on the level of the senses. Rather, let us emphasize the total, irreversible meaning of the word 'love.' Prostitution demonstrates once and for all the gulf separating sexuality and love."

Expressing love

It is, I think, all the more important to stress this contrast, since it enables us better to locate love in the fullness of its reality. Christianity is wholly centered upon the duty to love, whatever a person's particular situation may be.

If the sex act can find legitimate expression only in marriage—such is the unchanging teaching of the Church—other forms of expression can be appropriate in different circumstances.

Man is made to love and be loved. Our entire being tends toward love and desires to express love. The expression of love in intimate physical contact, whether or not complete sexual union is achieved, is authentic and true only within the context of married love—a consideration to which we will return. Outside this context, within which it attains its full potential, the sex act impoverishes man and destroys his capacity to love truly. And this is a tragedy.

A welcome evolution in the mores of today has rid us of some taboos and made the relations between men and women more natural, more genuine. Even so, a delicate balance has yet to be found between a past marred by

Jansenism and a present where in many instances restraint has been thrown to the winds. This balance can only be attained if attitudes are clear, and only if love and sex are unequivocally and uncompromisingly distinguished one from the other.

It is vitally important that the word "love" and the reality underlying it should be safeguarded in their purity and essential greatness. Christians—and especially Christian families—who experience real love, should not keep for themselves alone the secret of a joy found in fidelity to the law of God which is itself the law of love.

It is for them, especially, to publicly take all measures available to them to purify an atmosphere that is morally polluted, and thus save our younger generation for tomorrow. It is the future not only of married couples but the very structure of society which is being shaken to the foundations.

This effort to put things right presupposes that Christians are increasingly aware of what Christianity means for them and what precisely it is which makes a Christian a new being endowed with life by Christ, the redeemer and savior of men.

Living in Christ

Christian sexual morality is only a specific instance of Christian behavior grounded in the reality of baptism which should leave its mark on us throughout our entire lives. First, then, let us say something about this new reality bestowed by Christ.

If someone asks what difference, precisely, does it make to be a Christian, he should not be told that it is a matter of moral principles concerning which the disciple of Christ has something of a monopoly. He should be told, rather, that it is a question of a relationship with Christ, the Way, the Truth, the Life (John 14:6). Sometimes non-Christians fulfill better than ourselves the Lord's command: "Love one another."

To grasp the specifically Christian character implicit in the command of love, we must read to the end the words of Jesus: "Love one another . . . as I have loved you" (John 15:12). Jesus gives himself as the prototype of love. To follow his example gives our whole being a new dimension which, understood in all its demands, should lead to radical changes in our lives.

To the question "What added dimension does being a Christian bring?" one can rightly answer: "In a sense— as far as appearances go—nothing is added."

And yet, it has been rightly said that to be a Christian changes everything. At first sight these statements seem to contradict each other.

"But do we not find something the same in the case of those engaged to be married? What change has taken place in a young man who has become engaged? Has he become, by this very fact, more skilled in his profession? Has he become more intelligent? Outwardly no such change has taken place as a result of his engagement. And yet to be engaged transforms his life radically. Love has bowled him over. Or, rather, someone whom he loves and who loves him has come into his life. This realization is overwhelming: it changes his entire existence. The experience of the Christian who truly believes is something like this.

"How, then, have things changed, now that I am a Christian? Apparently nothing has changed. Whether I believe or not, the world around me will remain the same. And yet belief in Jesus Christ has transformed my life. Gradually I realize that God is interested in me: that my existence is precious in his sight. For did he not come to share our human condition?"*

*G. Ponteville: *Les nouvelles feuilles familiales*, 1976, No. 1

It is right, then, to speak of a new life. And this of necessity means new demands, an invitation to a new life-style and to a way of behaving which corresponds to this new birth (Eph. 4:1).

It is impossible to compress all that Christian morality implies into a code of rules. This morality is dynamic: it continuously engages us in new tasks, confronts us with new problems. It is the love of Jesus which urges us on to go to the ends of the earth. You cannot deduce from the gospel ready-made solutions to every problem.

However, this faith, this change of heart, will bestow a new moral power. It will give to all we do a meaning of another order.

The power of the Spirit, which does not exclude natural gifts, is inherent in all a Christian does. The boldness of Peter after Pentecost, the appealing wisdom of Stephen, the joy of the disciples—are human realities. But they are also, at a deep level, the working of the Spirit. In the light of faith this vitalizing symbiosis becomes experience of life, a sign of a Presence.

The Meaning of Chastity

The life-style required at every level by the logic of our faith finds expression in sexual matters in the practice of chastity, a virtue necessary in every sphere of life.

Today the very word has an antiquated ring. One hesitates to use it, so discredited has it become. Nevertheless, now, no less than formerly, its role is indispensable. It simply means that self-control must direct the sexual instinct if the latter is to be at the service of real love and integrated into its proper place in the development of the human person.

The Christian knows that this integration is difficult to

attain and that the imbalance in our wounded nature is particularly sensitive in this area. St. Paul complained of the tension he felt within himself: on the one hand, what he wanted to do; on the other, forces within preventing him (Rom 7:18-19).

Chastity is a matter of balance. It is the fruit of God's grace, and at the same time the prolonged efforts of man at grips with his own weakness and frailty. Chastity entails growth. Just as we are not born charitable or just, neither are we born chaste. We become chaste.

Chastity means liberating, for the sake of genuine love, that which is best within us. A virtue rooted in our baptismal mystery of death and life, which makes us the sons and daughters of God, it comes forth, like a flower from the stem. It is a response to the invitation of St. Leo the Great: "Christian, acknowledge your dignity and live accordingly."

Sin and salvation

The doctrine of original sin which we cannot deny—whatever may be the theological interpretations of this mystery—helps us to understand man's daily experience: an internal conflict of human instincts within him and around him. Our human nature, which is always with us, has indeed been wounded and is always vulnerable. The disorder throughout the world, the fruit of this conflict, is blazoned every morning in the columns of our daily papers.

Our natural instincts have to be controlled and channelled: violence, aggression, possessiveness, greed, and the like. Training is necessary. The exceptionally unruly sexual instinct needs to be formed, directed, put in perspective. Otherwise, man will become disoriented and will compromise his capacity for love.

But if evil unquestionably exists, if we have to acknowledge that we are wounded and sinful, we must also

27

be vitally aware of the redeeming, saving grace of God in Jesus Christ. Faith refines our perception and helps us to disclose traces of evil within ourselves. Chesterton said in his paradoxical way: "A saint is someone who knows he is a sinner." The scriptures speak of the Holy Spirit as of one who lightens our darkness, helps us to recognize it, judge it, and surmount it.

We find it hard to admit, not merely with our lips but in the very depths of our conscience, that we are weak in general. It is much harder still to admit to any specific fault.

Yet the same faith reveals to us the horizon of tenderness and grace within the heart of God, "infinitely greater than our own." St. John in his first letter invites Christians to acknowledge before God that if our hearts condemn us, God is greater than our hearts, and knows all things" (1 John 3:19-20). Faith encourages us to accept ourselves as we are, with humility and patience, knowing that the patience of God goes far beyond our own and that his love not only wipes out the past but heals it and creates us afresh to a degree beyond anything we could imagine. The pages of the gospel proclaim that Jesus came to heal the sick and those whom life has wounded.

If we doubt this, we have only to look at Calvary and see Christ upon the cross and so understand the profundity of his redemptive love at work for all time.

We live in a world in which the word "Savior" is becoming more and more infrequently coupled with the name Jesus. To know and to say that we are saved—not just in theory but in fact—we must realize that we are saved from something. Jesus came to save us from ourselves, from sin, from death, from the powers of evil. All this is devoid of sense for those who proclaim that man is self-sufficient, who deny sin, and dismiss as myths the hidden forces of evil. Jesus, whose very name means "savior," cannot be acknowledged as such if we are unaware of that from which we are saved.

I heard on television someone who regarded himself as a Christian exclaim: "I don't want to be saved. I want to be set free." The words overlooked the fact that salvation and freedom are closely united. Jesus, by saving man, through his life, death, and resurrection, laid the foundations for all kinds of freedom necessary to us. Christian freedom, which triumphs over sexual slavery, has been won at a great price. We must be cleansed in that current of graces which free us from ourselves, give us balance, and which, through the Church, continue to infuse the revivifying power of Jesus our Savior into our lives.

The sources of life

While Jesus remains the source of life and resurrection, we must live in close communion with him.

The Christian must accept humbly the laws of asceticism proper to a Christian. If today the Church no longer determines precise forms of asceticism, it rests with each Christian to introduce these into his life, in due measure, and in accordance with his circumstances. To be a Christian we have to pay a price. Also we have to be Christians along with others. Every Christian needs his brothers. Christianity is not something to be lived alone.

To respond to the demands of God in the delicate area of self-control, each person needs another person or a group of persons who can help and sustain him in his efforts in moral progress. We can only rejoice to see the upsurge of groups whose members help one another to journey together toward a deeper life of prayer as well as a mutual enrichment in the Christian marriage and family life.

A Christian, unless he risks contracting spiritual anemia, must be nourished regularly by the eucharist and by the scriptures which, for today as for yesterday, are the Word of Life. He must purify himself and allow himself to be healed through the sacrament of reconciliation. A tremendous effort toward renewal must be made. Moreover this calls for a fresh awareness of what sin is. And sin can only be understood within the context of the covenant into which God wills we should enter. A document published by the Belgian bishops in 1973* puts sin firmly in this perspective:

> If sin is always basically a breaking of the covenant, a refusal to love, it finds concrete expression in different forms of behavior opposed to the various demands that require us to be at one with God and our brothers. This opposition understandably varies in gravity in accordance with the values at stake and in proportion as the refusal is more or less radical . . .
>
> Strictly speaking, then, only those acts are sins which are concrete and "dateable" choices of what is evil. Wrongdoing cannot be reduced simply to a general, fundamental attitude comparable with the background on a canvas without the "pointillism" representing particular sins.
>
> In weighing the seriousness of sins, we must acknowledge man's formidable capacity to scorn the love of his Creator in transgressing knowingly and deliberately, in a grave matter, the demands of this love. Certainly such an attitude is not something trivial and vague. To claim, on the other hand, that

---

*Under the aegis of the Belgian bishops, a two-fold document was published by its theological commission under the title *'Orientations pour un renouveau de la pratique penitentielle. Reflections doctrinales—Reflexions pastorales'*. It contains useful material concerning the formation of conscience and the discernment of sin. I quote from para. 52-56 and 60.

this attitude is impossible, means in the last analysis—as someone has said—that we take seriously neither God nor man.

The effort to attain self-control in sexual matters, as well as in our shortcomings on the way, should be viewed in this perspective.

To sum up, the basic issue is a more or less deliberate and conscious choice for or against genuine love, for or against our living covenant with God.

Chastity in Marriage

At this point I would like to show how the universal obligation to be chaste can be applied in situations requiring a diversity of application.

First of all, the context of marriage. Love in marriage has to harmonize and integrate a number of elements, without, however, overemphasizing one to the detriment of another. For a long time the sexual dimension of human life and its importance in the growth of love were misunderstood or underestimated. Sexuality, in the broad sense, is what disposes each man and woman to enter into a loving relationship with another. Sexuality, before being an organic capability, is a "power for relationship." This dimension of the personality only develops in the true sense if supported by such precious human qualities as mutual understanding, openness, warmth, compassion and support one of the other. A failure to recognize this fact means the frustration of the Creator's hope for man.

Today there is a tendency to overvalue the physical side of sexuality and to isolate it from its total human context, thus giving it a priority to which it is not entitled. This is to falsify the significance of sexuality, for true love between husband and wife means an authentic, total, mutual relationship, a communion of soul, mind, heart, and body. It means that the two share and partici- pate in life together, at a deep level. And this entails a constant struggle against withdrawal into self, against the coexistence of two personalities travelling side by side, yet never really meeting.

The experience of the movement known as Marriage Encounter, which effectively helps thousands of couples to discover the deep reality of their life together, shows to what an extent husband and wife, if they would renew their love, must exchange a life in which they live in parallel for one that is shared.

Physical union finds its full meaning only if it is an expression of a personal communion between husband and wife.

Nothing is more fragile than physical harmony if it is not supported by the other dimensions of love. It is threatened by what Ricoeur called the "lapse into mean- ingless." The proportion of marriages broken by divorce—one in four in some countries—shows that the danger is far from being imaginary.

Hence the necessity of continually situating afresh the physical aspect of marriage within the context of a union in which each partner is acknowledged and re- spected in his or her totality.

For husband and wife, chastity is a virtue which gives freedom and value to the human person in the depths of his or her being. The physical expression of sexuality— as we know, we must distinguish between the sexual act and less intimate ones—is beneficial for man and woman in so far as it is at the service of life and love. This is the teaching of the Church.

As the Roman Document reminds us, sexual inter- course, for the Christian, finds its true human authentic- ity within the sacramental context of marriage. In this its rightful context, sex is an enriching source of joy and freedom for the couple.

Christian couples are invited to give to the world a living testimony of God's tenderness and creative love. All genuine love is "a giving of self" and creative of something new. Giving birth to and bringing up children is a privilege that evolves from this creativity. When this is not possible, the creativity that is inherent in marriage can find other forms of expression which also reveal the lavish richness of God's love.

Pope Paul VI, speaking to married couples,* summed up admirably the real meaning of the gift made by one to the other:

"The gift is not fusion. Each personality remains distinct. It is not disintegrated as a consequence of the mutual gift of self. On the contrary it is strengthened and refined. Moreover it increases as married life goes on, in accordance with the ennobling law of love: one gives to the other, that both may give together. Love, in effect, is the binding force which gives solidity to this life lived in common. It is also the inspiration that carries it forward toward an ever more perfect fullness. The entire being participates in it in the depths of its personal mystery and its affective, sensitive, bodily, and spiritual components, thus forming ever more perfectly that image of God that husband and wife are called upon to realize in their daily life, weaving it out of their joys and tribulations—so true is it that love is more than love.

"And love in marriage is no stranger to elation: a yearning for the infinite—a yearning, too, that this love may itself be total, faithful, exclusive, creative of life.**

* "Allocution aux equipes Notre-Dame," *La documentation catholique* (No. 1564). 7 June 1970, col. 503-504. Also in *The Pope Speaks*, Vol. 15, No. 2 (1970) Washington, D.C.

**Cf. *Humanae Vitae* No. 9.

"With this perspective, desire finds its meaning, its fullness. A form of expression, a source of knowledge and communion, the marriage act supports and strengthens love. Its fruitfulness leads the couple to ultimate fullfillment. They become, in the image of God himself, a source of life.

"The Christian knows that human love is good in its origins: that while like everything else in man, it is blemished and marred by sin, it finds in Christ its salvation and redemption. Besides, have we not the lesson of twenty centuries of Christian history? And how many are the couples who have found the road to holiness in married life, the one life lived together which is founded on a sacrament?"

Chastity Before Marriage

The Roman Document has drawn attention to the fact that sexual intercourse has its proper place only in the context of sacramental marriage. This reminder of traditional teaching runs counter to contemporary morals which regrettably are in a state of decline. The Church, anxious that some of her most precious treasure not be lost, cannot disclaim her responsibility to remind us of certain basic principles.

As Cardinal Marty said recently: "Human sexuality is at the service of love. It is a language between persons. It is a bond making possible communication and communion . . . Carnal expressions of love have meaning; they are charged with commitment; they are a harbinger of a common future; they call for a life of respect, fidelity, and joy; they offer a welcome to fertility; they are open to the gift of life; they participate in the work of creation; they bear magnificent witness to that solidarity with the future of the human family which we carry, each one of us, within us. Hence it is only in lawful marriage that these acts find their real meaning and moral rectitude."*

Sexuality and community

Human sexuality must always be lived in a human and, for a Christian, an ecclesial community which is always in the process of formation. It cannot ignore this context without sinking into individualism and, as a result, compromising the welfare of the social body.

We touch here upon the role of institutions (marriage in its social significance) as supports and guarantees of personal and collective development.

Here opens a wide field of reflection concerning the link today between sexuality and "public policy." We must see that the sexual area of life does not succumb to a blind permissiveness, the tragic consequences of which have been evident in social and economic spheres. It would be paradoxical, to say the least, if sexuality—an area in which the person is so intimately involved—were presented as a refuge for individualism. As if man were a social being only sometimes, when the whim takes him!

In an important declaration of the German bishops on Human Sexuality** the bishops wrote in the same vein:

"Many young people think that an engagement or a serious commitment justify sexual intercourse before marriage. In the teaching of the Church, according to which sexual intercourse is permissible only in marriage, they see either outmoded traces of a fear of sex or the suppression of human freedom in a deeply personal sphere.

*La documentation catholique, 4, April 1976, p. 334.
**La documentation catholique, 17 June, p. 579.

"To justify sexual intimacy which they take as a matter of course, they appeal to their good conscience. But for a conscience to be good it must also be accurately informed.

"A good conscience cannot be satisfied by the fact that a more or less large number of persons are acting in the same way. That is merely jumping on the bandwagon!

"What, then, is the right attitude? What is fitting at this point in their lives? We grant, certainly, that such a way of behaving is completely different from casual and unbridled sexual indulgence which is mere licentiousness. Nevertheless the fact remains that there are serious objections. Daily experience shows us that many engagements and pledges of love do not end in marriage. In having sexual intercourse these lovers behave as if they were married, when in fact they are not. Furthermore, contrary to what is frequently said, it is not possible by indulging in premarital sex, to 'try out' a marriage in advance. A personal gift of sex can only be given; it cannot be 'tried out.'

"Finally, in this premature sexual union, without the 'yes' which binds the partner, it is forgotten that the love of two human beings, to be genuine, should be concluded before God and before man.

"It is precisely in this field that many want to enjoy personal happiness without taking into account the form of married life which is required by the Church and by society. Marriage is a sacrament which raises to a higher level the bond of love between two human beings, making of it a visible image of the bond uniting Christ to his Church. There, we have a mystery of faith which we cannot explain in a few words. In the sacramental sign the gift of sex is likewise included.

"We ask young people who are thinking of engaging in premarital sex to reflect with sincerity on these points, to discuss them honestly and not to water down the demands of the gospel."

We can only endorse this earnest invitation and say once more that the subjective intention to enter into a personal relationship with another does not guarantee the moral rectitude of sexual intercourse. The country priest in the novel by Georges Bernanos said to the countess devastated by the memory of her dead child: "*We* didn't invent love. It has its own pattern, its own laws."

None of the aspects of human love can avoid being confronted with the principles which give to love its meaning. Far from being a mere source of pleasure, the human body is the *locus* through which man can express himself, as well as being for the Christian the "temple of the Holy Spirit" (1 Cor. 6:19).

We are all involved in a network of objective relationships the meanings and demands of which we must hold in respect. We cannot interfere—unless we are prepared to pay the price—with those imposing and fundamental symbols which Christ has raised to the dignity of "sacraments": efficacious signs, that is, of a meeting between God and man. The mutual gift of the body in the marital embrace is one of these.

Growth and integration

If love in marriage is a mutual love which tends toward complete communion in all its facets, it is important, if we really want to learn how to love, that the proper place for sexual values gradually be found.

Engaged couples should be aware that sexual progress must be sustained and supported by a like development of all the other values which contribute to the growth of the human person.

Marriage, the public institution which confers its social dimension upon the commitment of engaged couples, is not just a formality: for man to be a member of society is not something peripheral. Marriage is the public affirmation of a mutual responsibility being assumed, one for the other, by bride and bridegroom. It gives recognition, confirmation, and support to the "togetherness" of the couple who have come to the point of exchanging vows.

The real question to ask should never be: "How far can we go without infringing a law?" That would be to reduce the encounter of the sexes to something regulated by arbitrary laws dependent upon the contingencies of culture and environment. It is not a matter of reducing the area of what is permissible. We have, rather, to increase our respect for the growth of genuine love and the quality of life.

Such is required—or better, such is the Christian vocation—in the matter of sexuality which the Congregation for the Doctrine of Faith has thought fit to recall unequivocally: "Sexual union is legitimate only if the man and woman have committed themselves to a permanent life-long partnership" (No. 7).

Within a society which has too often trivialized and commercialized sex, the Church wants to protect man and to honor the sexual dimension of his life by refusing to admit that the gift of the body should be dissociated from a mutual commitment to freedom. The Church takes seriously the sexual responsibility of contemporary man; she reminds him that the moral order concerning sexuality involves values that are most important to human life. She protests prophetically against the obsessions of a permissive society, recalling that chastity is a means required by all true love (No. 11), that it "enhances the dignity of the human person and enables him to love truly, disinterestedly, unselfishly, and with respect for others" (No. 12).

It must be said again: the virtue of chastity—and it certainly does not mean just the "right use" of our bodies—is not out of date for anyone. It is, nevertheless, in danger of being seriously compromised in the cultural climate of today. Training toward self-control remains imperative. And no matter what anyone may think, self-control does not diminish a man: it is, indeed, essential to his fulfillment. Within the context of love, it brings with it a deep, natural joy.

The young who are engaged to be married, or who soon will be, are entitled to have the ideal of Christian chastity set before them. They should be told of recently acquired knowledge in the matter of sexuality. "The truth," the Savior said, "will make you free." To live, we need truth as well as bread.

Chastity Outside Marriage

In the present tendency to confuse love and sexuality, the latter is reduced to the immediate pursuit of a personal, easy satisfaction at the expense of the partner— even a consenting partner. This is one of the serious moral dangers that threaten our society, especially its younger members, thereby endangering the future. The marital act cannot be compromised with impunity nor indulged in prematurely, unless violence is to be done to some of our human values that most command respect. Such experiences are liable to undermine youth's capacity for idealism, generosity, and commitment.

Sexual union which is not within the context of total commitment and fidelity in love, at first sight resembles an act of love. In reality it differs as does a cut flower from a flower that is growing: the blossom that has been cut appears to be beautiful and alive, but, whether we like it or not, it has been condemned to wither—and quickly.

We must not deceive ourselves by appealing to St. Augustine's words: "Love, and do what you will." In their context the words certainly do not mean that any kind of "love" justifies any kind of behavior. Quite the opposite. They mean that the positive exercise of Christian principle can only be rooted in genuine love in accord with the gospel. Far from encouraging permissiveness, Augustine is urging us to examine the quality of our love and be sure that what we will is really an expression of this basic conviction.

It is not freedom which results from these experiences but enslavement—the decline in vital energy and its power for the future. The search for carnal pleasure outside God's plan and his will for man engenders slavery; this search is liberating only if it is within the context intended by God.

Masturbation

Apart from certain "experiences" of which we have just spoken, there is another in which sexual self-control must be exercised: masturbation. Whether masturbation be solitary or mutual, the Roman Document stresses the objectively disordered character of the search for carnal pleasure outside the context of marriage. At the same time it adds that there are considerations which of themselves permit, on an individual level, a less rigid evaluation of responsibility.

"Modern psychology," the document says, "offers much that is valid and useful to help in formulating a more balanced judgment on moral responsibility and in directing pastoral action along the right lines. It enables one to see how the immaturity of an adolescent (which can persist after adolescence), psychological imbalance, or habit, can influence behavior, diminishing a person's responsibility for his actions, with the consequence that he is not necessarily subjectively guilty of grave fault" (No. 9).

Moreover the text goes on to a principle long known to moral counselors of experience. It is good to see it put so clearly: "In the pastoral ministry, where it is a question of forming a sound judgment in precise instances, the habitual conduct of people should be considered in its totality not only with regard to the individual's practice of charity and of justice, but also with regard to the care shown by the individual in observing the particular precepts of chastity" (No. 9).

The Declaration recalls likewise the admittedly traditional distinction between "objective moral order" and "subjective culpability," "between sin and the moral subject." In sins of the sexual order it happens more easily, in view of their nature and causes, that free consent is not fully given. This means that in passing judgment as to a person's responsibility caution must be exercised. The words of the scriptures are relevant: "Man sees appearances, God sounds the heart" (No. 10).

Writing in *Love and Control* about masturbation in its obsessional form, I said that it was clearly symptomatic of a more deeply rooted disorder and as such needed to be looked into more thoroughly. "Often," I wrote, "a psychological block creates a sexual tension from which the victim finds release through masturbation. In getting rid of this 'emotional block' due, perhaps to disappointment in love or loneliness—the real task may be to detach the adolescent from himself and from an infantilism of which masturbation is a symptom.

"A positive education encouraging greater openness to others and inspired by charity—this, coupled with social interest and commitment, will help to get him out

of himself. It will enable him also to benefit to the full
from prayer and the sacraments to which every Christian should have recourse."

The unmarried life

There are many persons in the world who, for a variety
of reasons, are unmarried and so do not come into the
different categories which we have been considering. In
this wider context we have to include, I think, those who
are not married because they have homosexual tendencies. To all who, for whatever reason, are unmarried, it
should be said that every life can respond fully to the
Christian vocation to love: a vocation obligatory on all
regardless of the sexual element.

It is a mistake to think that love is linked inherently
with sex and that the absence of the latter implies a
defect or impoverishment. Genuine love can grow in all
its splendor and fullness in the lives of those who are
ready to respond to the particular vocation that evolves
from their state in life. Every life, it has been said, is
great if its predominant concern has been for others. We
must not allow a sense of frustration or failure to damp
our enthusiasm, cloud our ideals of love and service.

History and daily life provide countless instances of
those whose lives were wholly animated by love, though
pleasure in the sexual sense of the word was absent. Our
Savior, who is the very incarnation of love, is the most
striking example.

The charism of celibacy

It remains to say something about a form of voluntary
renunciation in the religious life: the charism of celibacy. I would like to draw attention both to its greatness
and its demands.

I would be guilty of a serious omission if in speaking of
sexuality I were to pass over the thinking of the Church
in respect of those men and women who, to respond to

the call of God and give themselves in much greater freedom, have renounced the married state.

Celibacy freely chosen so as to consecrate oneself exclusively, soul and body, to the Lord and the service of God's kingdom, can only be understood in relation to the mysterious call of the Lord himself: "He who has ears to hear, let him hear" (Matt. 11:15).

At the outset of such a choice as this, there is always, in one form or another, an inner conversation comparable with the one which took place between the Master and his disciples Peter and Andrew to whom he said: "Follow me, and I will make you fishers of men . . ." The response of Peter and Andrew is entirely positive: "Immediately they left their nets and followed him" (Matt. 4:19-20). It takes no other possibility into account. It is absolute because God is absolute.

Like every choice of a way of life, that of consecrated celibacy presupposes the recognition and affirmation that man is capable of committing his own future once and for all. Certainly there are risks in every promise and in the fidelity which it demands. But is not one of man's great qualities his readiness to face risks—to weave them into the fabric of an enterprise that calls for perseverance?*

The choice of a life vowed to celibacy is a wager. But a glorious one! Lived in the solidarity of the Church, it ought to leave one free to cry out to the world the priority of God, the greatness of his Kingdom that is to come, the richness inherent in certain acts of renunciation.

In these days when consecrated celibacy is under fire—often because the inspiration at the heart of it is not understood—we must present it in its true light. We must thank the Lord for having raised up such vocations

*See the pastoral letter "Commitment and Fidelity," pp. 6-16

in his Church. We must pray steadfastly that many young people will hear the Master's call and respond to it generously.

Consecrated celibacy is endowed with a wealth of grace that the Church will never allow to be lost—even if experience shows that we carry our treasures in vessels of clay (2 Cor. 4:7).

This treasure is indeed precious. We must take care to defend its rationale and our fidelity to it.

To know that we carry our treasure in fragile vessels is to be realistic. Better this than to behave as if we still lived in an earthly paradise, or as if human weakness in this sphere were nonexistent.

Fidelity to consecrated celibacy—as indeed fidelity to the Christian ideal of chastity in every walk of life— demands constant recourse to grace and to clear-sighted watchfulness over self.

Happily in our times relationships between men and women have become more direct, more natural. This has advantages, but it also entails risks. Experience regrettably shows that too often the failure to be true to one vocation can stem from the lack of reserve which sacred commitments require.

The vocation to celibacy for the sake of the Kingdom calls for an unqualified fidelity, which is characterized by particular delicacy and firmness. Although one cannot lay down hard and fast rules, a resolute refusal to compromise is essential. In all you do and say, let sincerity and openness reflect your true self. But be guilty of imprudence, and all is lost!

To overestimate your capacity to remain faithful to God and his demands, to let yourself be carried away by feelings—your own or those of others—to allow undue familiarity, all this is to put yourself in a false position which can only harm the spiritual life and, if you are not careful, lead to those defections which cause such distress to the entire Christian community.

Celibacy for the sake of God's Kingdom is meaningful only when it is embraced and lived wholeheartedly by one who sincerely wants to bear witness to this same Kingdom.

The priest who lives faithfully and happily his vocation to celibacy enjoys a grace peculiarly his own, along with a unique freedom to help couples—all couples—to build up and expand their love in accordance with the gospel. Families who welcome him and to whom he gives spiritual help are a support to him, showing by their very openness to his priesthood how much they need the Church, the sacrament of Jesus Christ—how precious, too, and enriching for the people of God, is his personal sacrifice. The joy and peace which he inspires, confirms, or helps to restore enable him to realize the deep spiritual richness of his ministry.

Both he himself and these families learn from experience that the sacraments and the charisms alive in the Church are complementary: they work together to build up the body of Christ and unite the whole people of God.

Conclusion

To close, I would like to convey to you a three-fold wish.

First, allow yourselves to listen to the word of God handed down through the living tradition of the Church. Do not assume a stance of stiff-necked opposition. Listen, rather, with a child's openness, to the Holy Spirit who gives life to the Church.

If we want to live the Christian life and to know what it costs and the joy it gives, we must allow the Holy Spirit to bestow upon us all his powers, his riches, his fruits.

We must be inspired and guided by the words of St.

Paul which the Pope himself quotes as "a kind of commentary on the Declaration":

> Do not conform to the ways of this world, but be transformed by the renewal of your mind, that you may discern what is God's will, what is good, acceptable, and perfect . . . Let love be without stimulation. Abhor that which is evil. Cleave to that which is good. Be affectionate one to another, with brotherly love, in honor preferring one another (Rom. 12:2; 9-10).

A Christian life which allows itself to be guided in this manner by the Spirit of the Lord will taste the fruits promised by his presence. St. Paul has listed the fruits by which the tree will be judged. They are love, joy, peace, patience, kindness, goodness, faithfulness, gentleness, *self-control* (Gal. 5:22-3).

In welcoming with all its demands the "love that the Spirit pours into our hearts" we will receive a "power of love" capable of transforming and giving life to every dimension of human existence (Rom. 5:5).

No one has lived this openness to the Holy Spirit at a greater depth than Mary, whom "the Holy Spirit overshadowed" in the dawn of the Annunciation and on the morning of Pentecost.

Mary offered herself to him, putting herself totally at his disposal, soul and body. Her openness to spiritual motherhood on our behalf remains for us—for our generation, too—a secret of purity, freshness, youth. Her unobtrusive, discerning presence dispels the darkness in and around us. She remains for ever, in the words of the poet: "Our Lady of the Brightness of God."

My second wish is that we accept our human condition in humility, just as it is, with its goodwill and weakness, courage and lethargy, and realize in all truth that the

Lord is for us, too, savior and redeemer.

The gospel, which is the gospel of truth, is furthermore—this we well know—the gospel of grace and pardon.

Whether our faults are objectively serious or not, we should read again the story of the Prodigal Son, not to follow him on his peregrinations, but, above all, to glimpse the depths of the Father's kindness and goodness. What matters to him first and foremost is not the son's avowal of his faults; the father is himself ready with his pardon when the son has scarcely begun to stammer his *"I confess!"* We can never stress sufficiently that the Father is much more deeply moved than is the son by the joy of reconciliation and merry-making.

We must, in humility, allow ourselves to be healed by Jesus. The gospel shows him to us in so many places tirelessly exercising his ministry of healing on those who come to him in faith. "Power went out from him" to heal every weakness, every infirmity, every sickness. This power continues still to work among us. To receive Jesus in the Eucharist is to welcome him who remains and will remain "for the soul as for the body" the resurrection and the life. To receive him in holy communion is to receive here and now a pledge in anticipation of what awaits us when man is transfigured in his entirety.

We must accept also, in humility, that we cannot live Christianity alone. We need our brothers who journey with us along the way. In the conflict which takes place within every man, first of all to grow up, then to remain faithful day by day to his most sacred obligations, he needs the support of his brothers. *"Vae soli."* "Woe to him who is alone!" These words of the scriptures have a particular truth in this struggle to maintain or develop self-control (Eccles. 4:10).

We know that God, who watches over us as a father over his children, will put on the path of each one of us the person or group of persons who will be able to speak in his name at this stage of life, at this crossing of the ways, the necessary and saving words. The scriptures tell us: "A brother helped by his brother is a stronghold." What tragedies could have been avoided if, at the hour of inner conflict and temptation, the words of a friend, a comrade, some close companions could have been spoken in time and taken to heart. An exchange of confidences helps so much to see clearly into oneself, dispel phantoms, put things into perspective.

At a time when emphasis is readily put on coresponsibility in our relations with higher authority, we must not forget that we are also coresponsible as to our brothers and that we can be guilty of faults of omission.

Finally, my third wish is in the form of an invitation to save real love from its counterfeits, from the deadly menace that looms over this sacred treasure in a world which has lost its moral bearings.

Restoring real love

We must go beyond the criticisms. We must listen to the basic message which the Roman Document offers. For my part I gladly subscribe to these words of Cardinal Marty which go straight to the point:

"Let us not use the limitations of a text as an excuse for ignoring the real issue which it raises. Are we going to allow human sexuality to be swamped in an immoral 'free for all' totally devoid of responsibility? Will our society still be capable of love tomorrow? How is it that our society succeeds in expressing only that within it which, in relation to love, is obscure, ambiguous, violent, and commercialized?

"Love is greater than all that. And the younger generations have only one desire: to save love from becoming meaningless.

"Yes, we must save love. Listen to the young . . . If they

48

speak out it is not always to revolt against prohibitions or customs, rules and principles. There is also their fear in the face of a life without love, in the face of a tragic breakdown in sexuality, love, marriage, and children. They will blame their elders for shirking their responsibilities . . . for no longer teaching them how to love.

"I could myself cite the experience of many families: those whom I meet; those who write to me. Yes, there are many families who live a life of love. It is demanding. It is sacred. It rejoices in the truth, as St. Paul says. (1 Cor. 13:6) Let them be heard, Let them speak out. Loudly."*

If the Christian is by vocation the leaven in the dough, it is the nature of this leaven to act on the dough to make it rise. That we ourselves live the demands of love is not enough: we must help to restore real love in the world about us.

The cheapening, the profanation of love is one of the factors, along with hatred, violence, and war, in which is demonstrated most clearly the action of these mysterious forces of evil and of the prince of lies, concerning whom the scriptures speak.

Christian families who live up to the demands of their faith—and of their love—have a special duty to affirm these demands both in public and in private and to search for concrete ways of fighting against the deterioration in morality at large in cooperation with others. May they have the courage to swim against the tide and combat all that cheapens love—in particular pornography as commercialized on the mass media. May they defend, too, the value of life from its very beginning, as they would the moral values which are the very foundation of any civilization. It is for them to remind the world of the truth spoken by the Lord when he said: "My yoke

*La documentation catholique, 4 April 1976, p. 334.

is easy, my burden light" (Matt. 11:30). This promise does not exclude suffering, but it confers a peace and serenity which the world does not know. May they proclaim the gospel of true love! If this, along with other demands of the gospel, runs contrary, today and yesterday, to opinions and ways of behavior, it is by no means surprising. Nor is it a reason for rejecting the gospel. In the "permissive society" of the declining Roman Empire it was principally in the matter of chastity that the nonconformity of the early Christian communities stood out.

Why should we allow ourselves to be unduly surprised that our perspective differs from that of many of our contemporaries? We would do better to acknowledge that sexuality is one of the spheres of the moral life where the gospel is at the same time most precise, most demanding, and most compassionate.

May Christians discover again that the law of the Lord is joy to the heart and light to the eyes. These words from the scriptures remain as true today as yesterday. We can and should repeat with the psalmist in gratitude:

> The law of the Lord is perfect,
>   reviving the soul.
> The testimony of the Lord is sure,
>   making wise the simple;
> The precepts of the Lord are right,
>   rejoicing the heart;
> The commandment of the Lord is pure,
>   enlightening the eyes.

(Ps. 19)

I conclude with these words of the scriptures, asking the Lord to bless you and, of his goodness, bring alive these pages which I write with all the love I bear you. Their sole purpose is to tell you that the Lord and his law remain for ever, for every man and woman among you, your source of life and hope.

The Christian

The Church in the
Face of Time

The Church in History

At present the Church is living through difficult times.
These are troubled because of the many issues raised,
but at the same time they are rich in hope for the future.
The crisis is obvious, but opinions differ as to its diag-
nosis. From where does it come, what is its nature, and
where is it leading to? The correct analysis of the symp-
toms of a disease must come before any cure; this is
unavoidable. As in order to orientate oneself at sea, one
must use a compass, know where one set out from, and
discern the currents and cross-currents that carry the
boat along or hold it back.

At the present time the Church is like a ship, exposed
to all the winds, knocked about in some Gulf of Gascony.
This situation is the result, on one side, of an exterior
factor: the state of the sea. The Church exists in and for
the world; she is, largely, the focus of unprecedented
changes which are spreading across the world. History,
in this second half of the twentieth century, is accelerat-
ing at a breath-taking pace; we change centuries every
five or ten years; it is a perpetual challenge to be taken
up.

There is also an inner factor, inherent in the ship itself,

which since the Council, has undertaken important readjustments, not in dry dock but in the open sea. The Church herself appears to be a dockyard in full operation; crew and passengers, each day, experience the extent to which their fate is identified, and how much life on board concerns them all.

And this is a new phenomenon too. The sense of coresponsibility of Christians has been awakened. There remains, yet, some distance to travel before disentangling all the consequences. But the opening has been made; it can only grow. This is the moment to recall the words of Victor Hugo: "there is nothing more powerful than an idea whose hour has come." For good or ill a new way of life is emerging in the Church.

We are coming out of a long period, too long, in which for many Christians to live in the Church meant the same as passivity and immobility, unthinking Christianity more sociological than personalized. Instead of accusing Vatican II, as some do, of provoking a flood after the thaw, it would be better to ask what caused the previous frozen state, which provoked the inevitable reaction, and how to prevent ice packs from forming in the future. The difficulties of our epoch are diverse and manifold. One of them is due to the fact that the renewal is spreading simultaneously throughout all areas of the Church's life.

Everything holds together. If, for example, one wishes to see the collegial aspect of supreme authority stressed in the Church, logic demands that the position of the bishop at the center of the local church, and of the priest at the heart of the community, also be reexamined from the same perspective. The priesthood of the faithful cannot be reevaluated without casting a glance over again at the ministerial priesthood, always irreplaceable, but capable of different expressions. The creation of permanent deacons and the giving of certain new powers to laymen obliges us to redefine our classical treatises and introduce a pluralism into ecclesial functions. Everything conditions everything else; everyone has to take up new positions in relation to his neighbor. All this is not accomplished at the wave of a hand.

The heart of Christianity

This presupposes, too, the ability to discern wisely what remains essential and what is secondary or peripheral in the heritage of the past. Our Christians—accustomed to receiving as a lump sum or sometimes mixed up together the pure gold of the gospels and the contributions of men—have not been prepared for this discernment. It is not easy to scrape down a Gothic cathedral, cluttered with baroque or modern stucco work, to lay bare the original arches. One does not leap at the title of restorer of cathedrals, in the manner of Viollet le Duc, without some previous knowledge.

In a text on ecumenism (the wealth of which has not yet been fully exploited) the Council used the happy phrase "the hierarchy of truths." All that is revealed is true, but not all is equally central. Precious bait for any ecumenical dialogue. So, too, is it for us all an invitation to distinguish what is at the very heart of Christianity from what is peripheral. *A fortiori* it concerns all that theologians, moralists, preachers through the ages have added of their own beliefs to the deposit of revelation, stepping too gaily across the threshold of mysteries. A tree benefits from being periodically pruned: by lopping off superfluous growth, one causes the sap to flow into the main branches. But, to maintain faith in the coming spring, one needs a sure hand not to cut into the quick, and a sturdy optimism before a tangle of dead branches.

The present renewal, so delicate to carry out and so exciting to live through, is still encountering a major difficulty: the very depth of the "conversion" which is asked of us. Being faithful to the gospel with all its demands, and at the same time being just toward the expectations of the world, cannot be achieved without suffering and contradictions. Life is made up of tensions seeking a balance: the discomfort of the move is the price to pay for discovering new horizons. The very depth of this work of the Holy Spirit demands time and patience.

But while we wait for the soldering together of generations and for the Holy Spirit to triumph over the sin which puts an obstacle in his way in each one of us, it seems to me that we would render a service to the present-day Christian, en route to the twenty-first century, by showing him that the Church is a reality planted in history. The moment in which we live is clarified if one links it to yesterday, waiting too to link it up with tomorrow—just as, in order to plot the position of a ship, one must measure the latitude and longitude on the map. Understanding the Church in relation to time in general helps toward understanding it in relation to our own time. There is everything to gain by seeing it thus, inserted into the heart of history, and not as an abstract reality, immutable and outside time.

Too long have we labored under a static vision of the Church, defined in terms of a juridically "perfect" society. Thank God we no longer see the Church through juridical categories but as a living reality which Christ animates with his presence and his life, and which pursues its way from the first Easter until the coming of the Lord, on a pilgrim journey through time and history, and advancing from stage to stage along an unfinished road.

The story of the Exodus shows us that God does not like giving surplus provisions to his people, but instead is ever on the watch to assure them their manna for each day. We have grown accustomed to accumulating many cumbersome acquisitions and to building for ourselves houses of stone and cement, instead of being content with folding portable tents and of keeping ourselves ever ready for the march.

A Church put back into history is more capable of urging her people to a greater readiness and suppleness, and of teaching them to be faithful, to the past, to the present, and to the future. This three-fold fidelity is the glory and the purest crown of the Church.

The Church and the Past

The whole being of the Church is rooted in the past. She is faithful to her origin; she is continuity and tradition; otherwise she denies her very nature. The Church is nourished by that fundamental continuity which ties her to her origin, as a tree lives from its roots. But one must beware of confusing her with the growths which spring up at the foot of the tree in the course of time. Certainly, it is not easy to distinguish what stems out of authentic dogma and theology from what is the result of the varying sociological and cultural situations. True theologians know this better than anyone and they are afraid of exceeding their limits.

What makes "conservatism" so sure of itself and so closed to dialogue is the extraordinary ignorance of history found among its supporters. They venture to dogmatize beyond the realm of dogma, and to canonize opinions which bear the mark and the wear and tear of their time, because they lack a historical perspective. Not only is history "mistress of life"; it is also a guide in research, simply because it places in context, makes relative where necessary, makes us modest and circumspect, balances one thing against another and places rails along the route, showing at the same time the potholes to be avoided. It teaches the art of working in relief and of keeping proportion. How many controversies would emerge from the morass if, on both sides, people were willing to take stock of the past, to go back to the sources, to search together for the complementary truths and the presuppositions that went unnoticed! If I really want to understand the direction and meaning of a past Council, I must get to know the situation with which the Council had to deal, its *Sitz im Leben,* its fears, worries, even its lack of knowledge. History is indispensable in helping the Church to remain truly faithful to her origins.

It even further enriches us. Over and above all this it teaches a lesson of humility and of confidence. Of humility, for it brings home to us in what very fragile vessels we carry our treasures. Of confidence too, for it shows us to what extent God is at work in the Church through the weakness of man. It makes us put a finger on the dilemma which Gamaliel long ago offered for the consideration of the court that wanted to condemn the apostles: either the preaching of these men is of human invention, in which case its end is near, do not worry about it, or it is of God and in that case do not set yourselves in opposition to him. That sort of apologetic is always of value.

Living tradition

To maintain continuity with the past is always for the Church a primary duty. From it, as we have said, she draws her sap, her source of life. The Church finds her earliest origin in the history of Israel; with the people of the Old Covenant, she travels back down the centuries. She has never allowed herself to be detached from this Jewish past, and she condemned Marcionism as a heresy, that advocated this split. If the Fathers of Vatican II were anxious to make a declaration favorable to the Jews, this was not only a matter of justice; it was the expression of the Church's fidelity to herself.

If her distant origin then is to be found with them, the Church's more immediate source is in the events of the last twenty centuries, events that are, at the same time and indissolubly, both history and mystery. These are the event and mystery of Christmas, of Easter, and of Pentecost.

The Church does not confuse history and historicism. She knows that her full reality cannot be measured solely by the methods of the historian. The very wealth of the objective reality we start from overflows all our departmentalizing; one can only approach such a reality in the light both of history and of faith. But the Church opposes and will always oppose any attempt at separation of the two. Never will she admit the distinction which some modern liberal exegetes—before, with, and after R. Bultmann—strive to introduce between the Jesus of history and the Christ of faith.

The decisive factor in the birth of Christianity is the historical Jesus of our Gospels and not the paschal faith of his disciples, even if these Gospels themselves do come down to us from the post-paschal Christian community. To make Easter a purely interior event, effected in the hearts of the disciples by some force whose unleashing no one has been able to explain successfully, is to misjudge the very foundation of faith. One can only rejoice to see the present growth of reaction against this interiorizing of the paschal mystery—a reaction even among the disciples of R. Bultmann, such as W. Pannenberg and the theologians of hope, about whom we will speak later. Christianity will never be reduced to a projection of the subconscious, collective or otherwise, to an ideology or to a dialectic. It is first and foremost an event, a person: Jesus Christ, acknowledged as Lord. The Christian is not a philosopher who has opted for an explanation of the universe, but a man who has experienced in his life Jesus of Nazareth, crucified one Good Friday and returned alive out of the tomb. The cry of Claudel: "Look, now you are someone, all of a sudden" is the cry of faith for all generations past and present.

However, if the Christian is a man who lives from the past, from a unique event of days gone by, he does not make contact with this past across a gap of twenty centuries; this past comes to him because it is living forever in the Church. When he said to his followers "Behold, I am with you, even to the end of all days" the Master meant to assure them of his presence in the Church and to wipe out between himself and us all the distance and remoteness with which the past is normally surrounded. In Christ the past has been overcome, surmounted. Because of him and in him the Church comes to us as the inheritor of a past that is vividly present. The Christian of today goes toward his Lord, not merely with his own personal faith, isolated and hesitant, but with the faith of the whole Church—of yesterday and of today.

He believes, as the inheritor of the believers of yesterday. At the moment of the breaking of bread the Church puts on our lips that magnificent prayer "Lord, look not on our sins, but on the faith of your Church." And it is with this ecclesial faith that I go to meet the Son of God. I believe with the faith of the patriarchs, of the prophets, with the faith of Mary and of the apostles, of the martyrs, the doctors, the confessors, the mystics and the saints. The strength of poor, weak Christians—which we all are—is to know ourselves to be in continuity as a link in an immense chain, joined with the Master by those who have gone before us in the way.

It is always, for me, a great moment when, during an ordination, the litany of the saints is sung. It is good to feel united to those ancestors in the faith, whose mediation we are imploring for the sake of the ordained. This communion, across the centuries, with the Church in glory is a fresh gust of wind, a tonic. It is like a pause on a mountain plateau: one breathes better there, because of the extended horizon.

In this chain uniting us to the past, there is a special, major link which governs our faith. "I believe," we say in the Credo, "in the Apostolic Church." That is to say that our faith is given life by the privileged position of the apostles, the witnesses. Built on the rock of Peter and on the Twelve as foundation-stones, it is here that the faith is anchored, from here everything is transmitted, and to here is everything faithfully referred back. The tradition which dominates everything, like a mountain peak commanding the countryside and dividing its rivers, is that which takes as its base the Word of God, lived and transmitted through the ministry of the apostolic college. What Paul wrote to Timothy, who is taking up his job, remains valuable for all time, "Keep before you an outline of the sound teaching which you heard from me, living by the faith and love which are ours in Christ Jesus. Guard the treasure put into our charge, with the help of the Holy Spirit dwelling within us" (2 Tim. 1:13-14). These words are imperative for any Christian who is essentially one of the faithful.

It is when the ship is blown about that we must offer to God and his Church a purer and stronger faith. Purer because resting on God himself and no longer on the sociological props of a Christian way of life that has passed, this reliance can be seen as personal, more committed more apostolic. Stronger, too, because one must know how to recognize, beyond and through the weaknesses of the Church, her true face.

In spite of the lines appearing on the face of his mother, an adult knows how to read in her expression, the eternal youth of a love that does not age. As children we believed that our mother had an answer to everything; as adults, we have discovered her limitations. But that has not diminished our life; it has strengthened it. As Christians, become adult, we know that we are indebted to the Church for the best of ourselves. That is enough for her to remain for us all, in spite of "her wrinkles," Holy Mother Church.

The Church and the Present

One would have a very truncated image of the Church if one saw her as only directed toward the past. She is preeminently a present reality. If the salvation of the world is a fact, accomplished once and for all on Calvary, redemption continues to be applied every day. Past and present interpenetrate: the past is made present before our eyes. "Christ is in agony through the centuries," Pascal said, "we must not sleep during this time." The mystery of salvation spans the centuries; it is visible before our eyes. When I give the host to a member of the faithful saying to him "This is the Lamb of God who takes away the sins of the world," I remind him that the Easter mystery is always at work.

The same is true of the immediacy of the gospel message. If the Church lives from the past, she is also entirely open to the present, to the *Kairos*. She offers God's message as good news which is equally fresh and new for each generation.

Lacordaire once defined the Christian in these marvellous words: "The Christian is a man to whom Jesus Christ has confided other men." These men, confided to us, are not men of yesterday, but of here and now; our neighbors in the street, our companions at work, our young people.

The study of and respect for the past does not imply immobility, nor archaeologism. The Church must always draw out of her treasure trove the new with the old.

She owes it to herself to be modern, incarnate, present in the width and breadth of human life, under all its aspects. The Council reminded us vividly of the need to read and interpret the signs of the times. *Vox temporum, vox Dei*. The saying is always of value. God still speaks today through events; but the living God needs to be put in constant contact with men of flesh and bone.

Relating God and events is a mission of mediation which the Church is daily called upon to do. It is not an easy task: every day new problems present themselves. The gospel is not a book of ready-made solutions; it offers the "words of life" that are relevant to the fundamental questions of man. It also offers a spring of living water, forever gushing forth. That is why the continual reading of the sacred pages in church remains a daily duty.

The Church must avoid canonizing the past. She must keep clear of any primitivism, which would consist in wanting to keep alive some past century as an ideal or a norm. There is no golden age to return to; we should not even hanker after the primitive Church.

We must not be mistaken about it either. The picture presented of these first Christian Churches had nothing idyllic about it and varies a lot depending on whether the background is Jewish or Hellenistic. A reading of Acts shows just how much the apostles felt free in regard to the "ways and means" to adapt to fulfill their mission. We must not copy, nor retrace, nor go backwards. It might be thought that, for the sake of ecumenism, a return of this sort should be undertaken: a return to the eleventh century before the Eastern schism, or to the sixteenth century before the schism of the Reformation, so as to resume the dialogue broken since then. No. The Holy Spirit has never ceased to be at work in the Church. It is from today and from the pooling of the wealth of grace of all different bodies that we must promote the visible union of the Christian Churches in a rediscovered communion of faith. We have not to undertake a work of restoration, rigidly transporting or projecting the past into the future. True development in the Church demands a growth in maturity.

As I grow up, my past always remains mine, but as it goes further away, I see it with new eyes. I am, now, something more than layers of the past, superimposed upon one another. Authentic tradition as opposed to pseudo-tradition is not the domination or hold of the past over the present, but is rather a living assimilation of the past in the present. In the Church's present the past is contained and at the same time transcended.

I find myself, at times, wondering, in imagination, what I would have been and what believed as a Christian, if instead of living in 1970, I had lived in 1870, in 1770, in 1670 and so on. This invariably ends in heartfelt gratitude to the Lord for the present time in which he has chosen I should live.

But if one must not yield to the temptation of pastism or primitivism, neither must one succumb to the mirage of "presentism" which is a sort of canonization and at the same time an abuse of the present. It is the temptation that awaits anyone who, in order to stress the duty of the Church to be present to the world, forgets or minimizes whatever is, and is always, simply an irreducible part of Christianity, independent of any age.

When in *Gaudium et Spes* the Council asks us to read the "signs of the times," it is not asking for the Church to be made worldly, adapted to whatever is of current interest or fashion. Nor was it simply an invitation to recast the eternal message into language accessible to all. It was an appeal to reread the gospel with faith, in the light of the Holy Spirit, and with the men of our time in mind. A rereading aiming to hear again the Word of God that is always living and contemporary. A readiness to grasp today "what the Spirit says to the Churches." Only is the Church faithful to herself if she remains always open to the surprises of the Holy Spirit, to the unexpected things of God.

What men, thinking or otherwise, desire above all is that the Church that they have before them should reveal the gospel to them. Our contemporaries desire to encounter the living Christ today. They long to see him with their own eyes, to touch with their own hands. Like those men of Palestine who approached the Apostle Philip to say to him: "We want to see Jesus," our contemporaries desire a meeting with him, in close contact. Unhappily for the sort of Christians we are, they ask to see Christ in each one of us; they desire us to let Christ be seen through us, as the sun through a window.

All that is opaque and grey in us disfigures the face of Christ in the Church. What the unbeliever reproaches us for is not that we are Christian, but that we are not Christian enough; therein lies the drama. Gandhi was very struck when reading the gospel. Indeed, he nearly became a Christian, until the spectacle of Christians deterred him and caused him to recoil. There, alas, is our heaviest responsibility.

The Church and the Future

This would not be complete without showing the whole Church as being in tension and expectation toward the future.

This orientation toward the future coincides, in an astonishing manner, with the concern of modern man— a concern so deep that he has created the sciences of prediction and of the future, to penetrate the years ahead that so fascinate him. Formerly, man sought to discover the secret of the future by studying the stars.

Today it is no longer a question of forcing an entrance into what is impenetrable, of guessing the future, but of creating it, of bringing it to birth, of inventing techniques that condition the march of progress. In the heart of the man of today, however anguished and uncertain, there is an immense hope seeking to find a way out. If modern man lives by a Messianic hope in time, the Church lives by a God-centered hope. She offers man a hope that "surpasses all that the eyes of man have seen, all that his ears have heard, which is none else but what God has prepared for those whom he loves."

Between modern man and the Church there is a meeting-point: their common concern for the future. Ernst Bloch, that influential Marxist philosopher, author of "Das Prinzip Hoffnung" wrote these words: "wherever there is hope, there is religion." The formula is ambiguous but has one valuable meaning to it. It is not astonishing that this same Ernst Bloch has enriched the thought of those theologians who have so strongly reaffirmed the eschatological aspect of the Church, the aspect of "the Church on a journey toward." It is of capital importance that the false opposition between the Church and the future be destroyed. We cannot let it be proved true that "the Church lives on memories, the world on hope." It is essential that the gospel be presented to the world as hope.

This concern of the world is not new. Kant some time ago posed the three questions, fundamental for man: what can I know? what ought I to do? what can I hope? His "Critique of Pure Reason," his "Critique of Practical Reason," and his "Transcendental Aesthetic" aimed at replying to this three-fold question. The third "what can I hope?" is to be found again at the heart of modern philosophy with a new pointedness.

In this way the Church rediscovers a dimension too neglected by Christianity, which is a journey, a pilgrimage leading to the Parousia, to the final meeting with the Lord. By stressing an openness to the future, the Church will recapture the ear of the young, turned as they are toward this world to be made, this tomorrow that each one glimpses, astonishing and ambiguous.

The world is henceforward in the hands of man—or almost. Nature no longer imposes itself on man as a sort of fatality, like some resistant building material, but as a supple matter that he can manipulate at his will and which he includes in his plans.

Modern man is fascinated by this world to be made. He is no longer fascinated by the ready-made world which he had to respect—at times in fear—and which only yesterday dictated its laws or was even hostile to him.

Far are we from the time of Philip II, King of Spain, who, wishing to make the River Tagus navigable, submitted his plan to a commission that rejected it, giving as a reason: "If God had wanted this river to be navigable, he would have made it so with a single word" and concluding that from henceforth "it would be a temerarious trespass on the rights of God if human hands were to attempt to improve a work which God left unfinished for his own inscrutable reasons." Our world is at the opposite extreme from such a way of thinking. We Christians have, somehow, to make connection between the transcendance of God and the future of the world without confusing God with some imminent worldly future as if he were at the term of a cosmic evolution, however complex. Everything that shows the Church en route toward her final destiny, toward the "God all in all" in the glorified Christ, carries a message of special attraction for our time. We have to return more and more to the God of the Bible, to the God of Isaac and Jacob, not to the God of the philosophers. We must detach ourselves from a philosophy inherited from Greece in which the universe was a world enclosed in itself, given over to a cyclic vortex with no vital impulse toward the future.

We have to rediscover the personal God of the Bible who is, first of all, not a God who wants to reveal propositions and theological theses, but the God of promises made for the future and who reveals himself to us as a love that is personal, gratuitous, first and last. In this perspective, the Church becomes better placed between the "already" of Easter and the "not yet" of the Parousia. In it too the past remains present and the future is already present; in it tradition is a perpetual renewal, evolution a continuity. In it lives the Christ of yesterday, today and forever.

The gospel will be an unparalleled force of life for the world to come if we can show it under this aspect. "A message becomes credible to the extent that it shows itself capable of opening up to hope and to the future." These words of Jaspers go far. There lies the credibility of the gospel, and the Church will be accepted and listened to, to the extent to which she can talk this language to men and translate their hope into joy. For joy remains the sign of the Christian: it is the certain test of the hope that is his, of that hope of which St. Peter said every Christian should be able at all times to give an account.

The world hopes for a gust of fresh air, a promised, liberating shout of Alleluia. Harvey Cox, when he published *The Feast of Fools*, made himself the spokesman for a powerful current of ideas and aspirations that is running at present. This book also is a sign of the times. It claims again a new place for joy, humor, fantasy, in a world replete with technique. Better than anyone, the Christian can answer this appeal. It is his job to reveal to men that joy is a flower that can only open and last in the nourishing soil of hope, which is born of God and finds fulfillment in him.

Charismatic Christians and "Social" Christians

During the year of reconciliation, we must attempt to relieve the tension which is polarizing two types of Christians: those who emphasize the spiritual dimension of Christianity, and those who make social action the priority. For brevity's sake, let us refer to them as spiritual or "charismatic" Christians and social action or "social" Christians.

In order to reconcile these two tendencies, we must clearly affirm, right from the start, that there is no such thing as a Christian who is not charismatic, since everyone who is baptized has been baptized in the Holy Spirit; and there can be no Christian who is not social, for that would mean a member who is amputated from the body of Christ. In all honesty, there should be no problem for those who accept the gospel, the entire gospel, word for word, without omitting those texts which complement one another. Nonetheless, each person will develop an approach to the gospel which characterizes him, and will see the relationship of God-world-Church-world in a different perspective, according to his own particular point of view.

We know how very necessary are both perspectives, the social and the spiritual, to achieve the desired reconciliation: they are complementary, and one cannot do without the other. Our perpetual temptation—hence our tensions—is to interpret our complementarities in terms of opposition and to pronounce exclusions—"excommunications" in the sense of "rupture of communion"—where in fact we ought to be welcoming, open-armed, the richness of vision which the Lord asks of his disciples. I will not venture to describe in detail each of these tendencies, for the simple reason that each one will refuse to let itself be categorized, on the reasonable grounds that to categorize is to distort its own thought. This is a good sign and invites an optimistic response on our part. The dialogue between "spiritual" Christians and "social" Christians brings up the old problem of "contemplation versus action" and, if you wish to delve deeper into the dilemma, "faith versus works." That would bring us back to the ancient theological debate between the Molinists, accentuating man's liberty and the freedom of his role, and the Thomists, or "Banesians" who emphasized the sovereignty of divine grace and its priority.

We know that one pope, Clement VIII, invited partisans of each tendency to explain themselves in public debates. Consequently, there arose the famous dispute, *de Auxiliis*, pitting Jesuits against Dominicans, which was ended by the intervention of Paul V, closing the 45-week-long debates and forbidding—under pain of excommunication—the reopening of this unresolved theological quarrel. But for our purpose here, it is not necessary to go so far in the presuppositions and preliminaries. Let it suffice us to find the roads which will bring us together, the pathways that will join us harmoniously.

In short, the eternal debate is found in the initial perspective, and often exposes itself unconsciously. You will have two differing points of view, one of which is chosen above the other. The "volitionist" option can be simply summed up as: I act, I take initiative, I forge plans and, of course, I count on God's grace to support my action. The other prespective which sounds the preliminary overture to God is: Lord, what would you have me do? Guide me, step by step, so that I may enter into your plan, into the mystery of your will. Help me to cooperate with your working in my life. Be it done unto me according to your word.

Now let us return to our two types of Christians. First, we turn to those who wish that evangelization would begin with man's problems and temporal commitments—political and social—which form his daily life, for we need to recognize the validity of this "incarnate" or social approach. The "pietism" which has been isolating prayer from action still remains a danger, and the logic of prayer translates itself into effort for the transforming of the world, to begin with the "worlds" that surround each one of us in concentric circles. We have no right to ignore the traumas which torture men: even now, the world economic crisis; the control of economic systems which reduce men to mere statistics in their calculations of profits and losses; the ever-worsening problem of unemployment—all of these things demand our attention, and concerted effort. All social commitment which aims to remedy and assuage the disquieting situation is a human as well as a Christian concern, and imposes itself on us necessarily. One could cite numerous pages of the New and Old Testament to point out the link between love of God and love of one's neighbor, between the first and the second commandments, without forgetting that superb text on the Last Judgment where the Lord identifies himself with our neighbor in order to judge us (Matt. 25:35-45).

Now let us consider an approach initiated by God. He has revealed it to us in Jesus Christ, by a completely free invitation—beyond our hopes—unforseeable and unsettling, demanding on our part humble acceptance in faith.

It is only natural that the first commandment be ranked first, not merely because it concerns our loving God in himself and for himself, but also for ourselves, for the sake of our Christian conscience. The first commandment leads us quite naturally, by its internal logic, to the second commandment.

To put God in the foreground does not mean that we fail to recognize the urgent needs of society. It is the number one social service that we can and must perform for a society that needs to discover—and rediscover—its axis and fundamental equilibrium.

We are familiar with the allegory by Hans Christian Andersen about the spider who, having spun a magnificent web, wanted to free itself from the thread which attached the web to the branch, thus breaking a connection which appeared to the spider superfluous. This caused the web to collapse, for it destroyed the central cord of cohesion and unity. It is the same with the society of human beings, centered on God. Adhesion to God creates social cohesion: the vertical line is essential to the strength of the horizontal connections.

Putting God in the foreground also helps us recognize that the evils of society are not only institutional, but they are born—under any kind of system—in the heart of man, in his self-centeredness, in his sin. The "quid leges sine moribus" is as true as the inverse proverb, "quid mores sine legibus." "What good are laws if morals fail?" "How can morality be promoted if the laws will not support it?" As the German theologian Heribert Mühlen recently wrote: "Changing man is as important as changing man's structures and it is impossible to pit one against the other."

We could go on and on. I simply wish to tell "pneumatic" Christians: You have understood the meaning of prayer and I rejoice that you have entered into the Upper Room. Jesus had told his disciples that they must wait for the coming of the Holy Spirit at Pentecost before going out to preach the Good News to the world. Transformed by this Holy Spirit, a nuclear energy was released in them and dispersed through them. But it is not sufficient to *enter* the Upper Room; you must then go forth from it. Authentic prayer will never be an escape. It must become action; love of God must necessarily become love of others. Prayer must become creative imagination, love, compassion, justice, and reconciliation.

To those who feel as priority the urgent need to rescue a world in distress, I would say, yes, go ahead; but first, go into the Upper Room. You are powerless by yourselves; it is first necessary that a power from on high overshadow you. Without it, you will stumble on your way, and be overwhelmed by the task of rolling away the stone which covers the tomb.

In closing, two names come to mind which, for me, incarnate this indissoluble union between prayer and action. No one will deny that these persons are "social" Christians; and those who know them know that their action finds its source in prolonged contemplation, in continual prayer. The persons I am thinking of are my friend Dom Helder Camara and Mother Therese of Calcutta. Her words stir even those who do not understand a single syllable of them, for they sense, when she speaks, something beyond humanity, in the beat of a human heart. We need complete Christians—invaluable Christians—like these two. The Church, says the Orthodox theologian Meyendorff, must truly become herself again, and not merely change her outward appearance.

May we rediscover that deep source which alone can quench man's thirst, that gush of living water of which

Jesus spoke when he cried out in the temple: "If any one thirst, let him come to me and drink. He who believes in me, as the Scripture has said, 'Out of his heart shall flow rivers of living water.' This he said about the Spirit, which those who believed in him were to receive" (John 7:37-38).

What Can We Do to Overcome Unnecessary Polarizations in the Church?

The title of this essay implies the existence of a permissible borderline area open to various inescapable tendencies and emphases. But the essential problem is one of preventing these phenomena from ossifying into a kind of sectarianism instead of sharing in a fruitful interactive process. In short: How can Christians live in sincere intercommunion when they allow themselves to be divided and subdivided for the sake of a whole range of different suasions?

I see only one way of solving the problem: an unceasing concentration on the very foundation of Christian community—our common, living union with one and the same Christ, the Lord and Master of our whole life. For I believe that the answer is to be found in experience itself. Mathematics tells us that two quantities equal to one and the same third quantity are equal to one another. In the Christian perspective, we have to put one basic axiom in first place: Christians will be one, despite all that now divides them, in so far as they respond deeply to the challenge of Christ and his gospel; in so far as they can empty themselves to leave room for Christ as their unity, through them and beyond them as well as in them.

Christianity is not primarily an "ism," an ideology or a system. It is the encounter in Jesus Christ with the living

God. It postulates the wholehearted living of his basic demand, which is love of God and of one's fellow men; a process which "begins at home." Paul talks of a priority of reciprocal love for the "*domestici fidei.*" That is the primary condition and essential atmosphere for any attempt at union.

Patriarch Athenagoras always insisted, in ecumenical discussions, on that "dialogue of love" which is the wisdom of experience and the "short way" to visible unity. But this actual and reciprocal love must not turn in upon itself; into, as it were, a mere enlargement of the ghetto. As Saint-Exupéry said, "Love doesn't mean looking at one another, but looking together in the same direction."

What we need in order to overcome centrifugal forces is a common perspective on God, and a common perspective on mankind. A truly Christian form of communion and community is like the Saint Gothard tunnel between Switzerland and Italy. To get rid of our conflicts and all the blocks obstructing the tunnel we must have a double intake of fresh air.

In regard to God, the common Father of all the faithful, it is a question of opening ourselves to him by listening to his word. We have to open ourselves up in common to the message of the gospel; to allow ourselves to be re-evangelized and re-christianized. There is no escaping this demand. We are all, more or less, "sociological" Christians, heirs to the narrow-mindedness of past and present. We have to do a bit of spring-cleaning in order to get down to the evangelical substrate, right under all those encrustations produced by the accidents of history and men's sinfulness. We have to rediscover our primeval and fundamental origins.

This common perspective on God implies listening to God; opening ourselves up to him, and prayer in common. We have to relearn continually how to say the Our Father honestly, loyally, and together. We have to relearn the breathing into us by the Spirit of that unutter-able prayer which he alone inspires. I am sure that the charismatic movement now evident in the Catholic Church and other Christian Churches could be of great value in teaching Christians that true prayer which gives unity by virtue of the Spirit. Very often those prayer groups which come out of this spiritual move-ment bring together Christians of all denominations. For me they are a practical demonstration of an essential unity eluding and cancelling polarizations.

Unity is also necessary in a common perspective on man. We have to respond together to the challenge of the same difficulties and the same hopes of an expectant mankind. This opening up to the world in general rel-ativizes all of us; that is, it gives us a new ratio, a per-spective which discloses the main issues of the moment and requires us to concentrate on the essential message of the gospel.

The Church cannot turn in on itself and cannot identify itself with the Kingdom of God. But it does have to bring nearer its hour and its advance. Common action among Christians is a sure path toward unity, even though it may not bring about full communion in faith as such. One condition, of course, is that it does not lapse into mere social pragmatism.

This common action is also one of the surest means of discovering one another in truth and of really listening to one another. Such a form of listening is rare because it asks for self-emptying, and wholehearted attention to others; and because it has to be learned gradually.

One has to know how to listen to what is said, but much more often to what is not said: the unvoiced presupposi-tion or subsidiary postulate. Words must be used to get to the deep intention. It is essential to go some way with the others before any discussion. If you want to convince someone else, he has to be sure that he is understood, that we have taken in that part of the truth which interests him and which he sets up against us. All men want to be understood in their best parts. As Paul VI said in an address to the Secretariat for Non-Believers: "No dialogue is possible without a deeper understanding of the partner in dialogue, or, as they say nowadays, of the other. This valuable task requires generosity and true asceticism. We have to go beyond the limits imposed by all languages, cultural reflexes, and even polemics and distrust in order to open up to abandonment of self and to universality" *(Documentation catholique,* 20, 1972, p. 959). Theologians have already made a serious attempt at reconciliation in the form of the post-conciliar ecumenical dialogue. Fruits of this authentic form of mutual listening are already available—for example, the common documents on baptism and the eucharist. It is desirable that members of the same Church should find the right common wavelength so that we can overcome our exclusivisms. It is high time for us to rediscover brotherly unity among Christians; that unity required by the Lord as the very test of our credibility in the world.

Once unity happens at the requisite depth, the process of opening up to contrary tendencies will become complementarity. It is not diversity which is wrong, but diversity which ossifies as exclusiveness and refuses to yield to full communion. A diamond is enriched by its many facets. The one light is fragmented. In God, variety is as supreme as unity. Each man's relation to the other is constitutive and congenital and the triumph of his own personality. Reciprocity resides in God, who is undying love. All talk about Christian unity is enlivened by the mystery of the Trinity, which is its source and image.

Who Is She?

In a liturgical prayer, this admiring question is asked by the angels—charged with welcoming Mary into heaven: "Who is this coming forth like the dawn, beautiful as the moon, bright-shining as the sun, awesome as an army arrayed for battle?"

Not only angels, but men as well inquire about her. Today's Christians make no unanimous response. Protestant Christians contest her place in the economy of salvation; certain Catholics believe they must minimize her role for the sake of some vague concern for ecumenism.

In order to derive the more accurate perspective, we must, before all else, enter into God's own thought and plan for Mary, and discover the role and place he has destined for her. For that is what matters above all else: What is she in the eyes of God? Why did he want her? How was she to function in his plan of salvation?

God's design

True devotion to Mary comes not from below but from above. It is commanded not from emotionalism but from faith; it is, first of all, adhesion to God and the accepting of his designs. Such devotion belongs integrally to our straightforwardness of intention with respect to God.

For Christian recititude begins with voluntary adhesion to God's plan, by rallying to him who directs his grace as he sees fit. God wanted to associate Mary with his work of salvation. Through her, he gave his Son to the world. God does not revoke his gifts, and this "order" is set. Mary's mediation lasts forever; that is God's design.

Jesus Christ always did the will of his Father. With such love did he enter the world by the path which his Father designated! We his disciples must not hesitate to similarly receive Mary as he himself did. Since it was God himself who chose her for his Son and for us, it is not for us to choose, but to receive her as our mother. Her beauty and her goodness attract us; we sense a need to run to her. But we are happy to first submit ourselves, in obedience, to the will of God. This is the principal reason why we express devotion to Mary. It is not for us to define the limits of divine action or to bypass the intermediaries God has freely chosen. It is characteristic of God to love us superabundantly and to communicate to his creatures the glory of being his instruments. In God there is room for all sorts of luxuries, yet it is we, in our human situation, who economize. Our relating to Mary as our mother is nothing less than grace in action, bestowing upon us divine love of which she is a permanent and living witness. It would be a serious mistake to consider devotion to Mary a useless addition to our faith, hindering our relation to God.

This devotion to her is not something extraneous; neither is it a concession to the imagination and to popular sentiment, nor a short-cut to salvation. For each one of us it is an expression of God's desire for our salvation.

Mary is both a channel to God and a gift from him. This divine will contains a mystery of love. For Mary, after her Son, is the most outstanding grace of God. "Oh, if you only knew the gift of God!," Jesus said to the Samaritan woman. Within this gift is enclosed the gift of Mary because this mystery of the Son encompasses that of his mother. We must not hesitate to accept her who is offered to us from God's hands. To each one of us, God says in some way what the Angel said to Joseph: "Don't be afraid to take Mary to yourself . . . that which is in her is of the Holy Spirit." We must humbly receive this gift from on high; we need to accept wholeheartedly all the love God has invested in Mary, for her sake and for ours. All that is necessary for us to know is what God desired for her and through her. St. Paul said that every Christian receives grace "according to the measure of Christ's gift." What is the measure of this grace in Mary? That is all we should want to know in order to love her as God loved her. So we look to God and nowhere else for the answer.

The laity should not be surprised that theologians have far from finished their study of this mystery. The theologians fill an indispensable role; they examine the whole of our faith, taking an inventory of the riches and harmonies therein, shedding light on truths side by side, in an attempt to synthesize it all. They also arrest extremisms or fantasies resulting from exalted or off-centered piousness which might carry us away. It is all this that Vatican II wished to recall in explicit terms.

Far from being scandalized over certain conflicting theological convictions, we must recognize in them a common effort to more deeply penetrate God's thought as it expresses itself in written and living tradition. Just as the cathedral builders raise flying buttresses and arched vaults against one another, so do theologians work together at a common task in the Church, even when each one emphasizes complementary truths. They are collaborators, sometimes unwittingly, in an ecclesiastical task which overtakes and unites them; they serve the Christian community and hierarchical Magisterium from which comes decisive teaching, authentically guaranteed. For example, take the evolution of dogma on the Immaculate Conception, where theologians persisted in defending either the universal redemption of humanity by Christ, or the privileged anticipated redemption of Mary. This illustrates what we were saying about doctrinal thrusts which the Church guides at the moment God has chosen toward a superior synthesis by drawing one-sided views together. It just so happens that the supernatural instinct of the faithful precedes the explicit and always laborious formulations of dogma. This simply proves that the Holy Spirit, according to the Master's promise, is at work in all his children, the humblest as well as the most scholarly. But we should be grateful to theologians for having, with their figurative dams, raised the level of water, thus reinforcing a stronger current. This all counts as gain for the full truth.

The Mystery of Mary

Scripture tells us how Moses, on coming to Mt. Horeb, saw the Angel of the Lord in the form of a flaming bush. Moses looked; the bush burned but was not consumed by the fire. He wanted to come closer to examine this sight, but God's voice, calling from the center of the bush, ordered him: "Don't come near; take off the shoes from your feet for the place on which you are standing is holy ground."

Tradition has often compared Mary to this flaming bush that burns without being consumed. A mother, yet virgin, she carried this flame of fire, the living God. The presence of the Lord in Mary makes her a high place of holiness, a sacred ground which can only be approached with infinite respect, stripping ourselves of views too human.

We are entering into a world which is not of familiar dimensions; we are penetrating this kingdom, God's kingdom of unfathomable love. Most certainly, Mary is a creature; by herself she is nothing, like all the rest of us. One need not insist on this, for it is obvious. The love of God invaded her, like a torrent gushing in a whirlpool. The Church throughout the ages owes it to herself to measure still more accurately the height, depth, the breadth of divine love at work in Mary. One cannot approach this mystery without grace, without enlightenment from the Holy Spirit, "who alone probes the depth of God," and who advances, like the High Priest of the Law, from behind the veil to the heart of the sanctuary. To know her, it is necessary that grace produce a certain affinity in us, and purify our regard. "He who loves not, does not know God," says St. John. This is true for Mary, too.

It is not surprising, then, that through the course of time, those who have brought us the best understanding of Mary have been saints. This serves to confirm Christ's word that it always pleases God to "reveal these things to the little ones and the humble." All that modern philosophy teaches about the interference of the heart's dispositions and the mind's lucidity is true in this domain more than anywhere else. A certain freshness, purity, and delicacy are needed to enter into this kingdom of light and of love. One saint who entered into it more in depth called Mary "God's paradise; his indescribable world." He affirmed that God made a world—our world—for man in transit; and he made one for the blessed—paradise; then he made one for himself, named Mary. That is not mere lyricism, but an affirmation, maturely reflected upon, which can help us understand why Jesus consecrated thirty years of his life to increasing endlessly in his Mother the fullness of the grace, initially granted to her, for the glory of the Most Holy Trinity.

This same holiness explains why the mystery of Mary only reveals itself a little at a time. Each of us individually, and so the entire Church, will gradually discover this, but it will be a slow and progressive realization during history.

Divine revelation ended with the death of the last apostle, St. John. But our awareness and understanding of revelation, through the illumination of the Holy Spirit, grows and intensifies throughout the ages. This awareness can be compared to the successive discovery we make of certain stars. The stars have, of course, existed since their creation long ago. But we only become aware of them as their light reaches us after centuries of travelling. In the same way, Christ himself revealed something to us about the nature of his truth when he said to his apostles: "I still have many more things to tell you, but you cannot bear them now. When the Spirit of Truth comes, he will guide you into all the truth" (John 16:12). Thus, Jesus left it for the Holy Spirit to lead the apostles into the fullness of truth. God entrusts this progressively deeper grasping of religious truths, not only to the quest of knowledge enlightened by faith, but also to love, or more exactly, to loving intelligence, propelled by the heart and vitalized unceasingly through practice and action.

Love is not juxtaposed with the work of the mind; it stimulates the mind from within; it always encourages the investigation and possession of what it loves. Love wants to read from within; love aspires to know intimately; love wants to coexist with what it loves, espousing all the contours, examining all the folds, to learn the ultimate secret of existence. Love is not satisfied as long as it is not able to read an open book, nor as long as a single reaction escapes it. Love exists at each moment like the gambler who puts his whole fortune at stake. That is why love wants to know everything, explore everything, explain everything, since, according to Pascal, you can't really know someone unless you know everything about him.

Love and truth are so intimately mingled that we cannot approach one without the support of the other. It is only natural that their parallel and unique pathways mark even the developmental stages of our religious quest.

Love is not merely sentiment; it is also determination and faithful action. To love is to translate into action what one has in the heart; it is to render real and effective our will to do the good. Maurice Blondel notes with unusual alacrity: "Faithful action is the ark of the covenant, wherein dwell the secrets of God. What Christ longed for was not to be analyzed like a theological theme, but, more than anything, to be loved."

In closing, let us return to the original question: "Who is she, this Mary?" We have showed at what point the question is beyond answering, so much and so great is God's magnificence in her.

Who is she for God the Father?

She is his daughter who is privileged for so many reasons. She is, from the beginning of the world, in Christ, his first thought and his first love. She is, from the first moment of her existence conceived in grace, one in whom the Father is well pleased. She is associated with the Father through the birth of Jesus: whereas the father engendered him eternally and as God, she gave birth to him in history and as man.

Who is she for the word of God?

She is the one whom Christ chose to be his own mother, the one whom he prepared from all eternity for this unequalled task.

An artist across the Atlantic, being congratulated one day for a very successful portrait he had done of his mother, replied to his admirers: everyone paints his mother "just as nice as he can."

It is a law of the human heart. Mary is the masterpiece of the Almighty. It is also a law of Divine Providence, which is always at work preparing those whom God calls. "If God seizes one of his elect," wrote Father Régamey, O.P., "to make him into a prophet, he purifies his lips with a flaming coal, for from his mouth will come God's oracles; if he raises up a precursor, he sanctifies him, from the time he is in his mother's womb; if he founds his Church, he establishes it upon a rock to which he gives a consistency adequate to communicate his purpose to all those who will seek support in that Church. The examples of Isaiah, John the Baptist, and Simon Peter should suffice to demonstrate to us this law of divine ways; there is not one single case presented in scripture that does not verify this in detail: God doesn't take just any instrument for his work; he prepares and adapts his chosen instruments." Mary is the one whom the Son of God raised to her unique role as Mother of God.

Who is she for the Spirit?

She is the one whom he flooded with sanctifying grace even from the moment of her birth. It is she whom he overshadowed at the Annunciation, when by his power, Jesus was conceived in her womb. It is she who, in the Upper Room, presided over the outpouring of the fire of Pentecost, which the Church was to carry to the world. She it is in whom the Spirit produced Jesus Christ, Chief of the Elect, and through whom the Spirit will continue to produce Jesus in the faithful elect until the end of time.

Who is she for us?

She is one whose entire destiny is to hasten the coming

of Christ. For all men, she is Our Lady of the Coming, for all the baptized, in whom Christ is already born but in whom he must still grow to attain his full stature. She is also for all who have not yet discovered the Savior, for these well-intentioned souls who search gropingly in the night, but who have not yet understood the signs in the sky. She is also for those who, if they have seen the star shining, have not yet found the courage to leave their native country, to journey forth bringing gold, frankincense, and myrrh to his feet. She it is who calls us to the service of her spiritual motherhood toward our contemporaries; she who demands our lips, our hands, our whole selves in the service of her Son, to be with her "Christ-bearers," carrying Christ to men who are dying because they ignore him.

Where Do We Go
From Here?

Journalists have asked me, over the years, a lot of questions, sometimes very tricky. What do you think about the pill? abortion? population problems? Women's Liberation? Never before have I been asked this very serious question: "What is the meaning of life after death?" But this is what everybody should ask, in the depth of his own conscience, because this question means, finally: "How do you see life today?" The future is not only the future; it is the key to the present. I have to make an option, a choice.

May I tell you, in a few words, the story of my own vocation to the priesthood? As a little boy of seven or eight, I remember I was very struck with the idea of eternity. I was impressed by the words of some speaker, explaining, with all sorts of examples, what eternity meant. It meant the end of time and space, it meant always, always. I repeated that word to myself, and it gave me, forever, the impression that life here on earth was so short a thing that, even if it was for 80 or 90 years, it was as nothing in comparison with that "always." I decided to opt for eternity, and to make the best of our short life to prepare for eternity. As a consequence, I felt the call to become a priest, with the idea that the best way to obtain a wonderful eternal life was to prepare many others for that life to come, for that everlasting life, by bringing to them the gospel as the way to eternity.

If nothing was to be expected after death, for me life would have lost sense and meaning. I cannot understand either suffering or love if I cannot see both in the light of eternity. Suffering cannot be without meaning. Suffering cannot be just nonsense. Let us imagine a child in the womb of his mother. Let us suppose, for a moment, that that unborn child should become conscious before birth. What a chaos of impressions that child would have! It would all seem so meaningless. But all that apparent nonsense receives a meaning the day the little child is born, and sees the sunlight. Then it appears clearly that every moment of his growing in the womb of his mother was a novitiate for life, preparation for the future.

In the light of eternity, meaning the new life after death, I cannot yet explain everything, but at least I feel the meaning, the orientation, of all that. If life here on earth is preparation, a novitiate, then I come out of darkness and see a ray of sunshine in all that happens to me. In the same way, I cannot understand love, real love, true, deep love, without the perspective of eternity. I refuse to love and to be loved only for a short time. True love involves, in the heart of each of us, that love will last for ever and ever. Every song of love will have some way of expressing that. "I will love you always." The human heart cannot be deceived in this.

That future is a light for life and present time, and this should be enough for us: this is what we essentially need to know. But, of course, we wish to have at least a glimpse of that future, and to get some idea about where we go from here. The question was put to a philospher, when he was dying: "What do you feel now?" His answer was: "An immense curiosity." I hope my answer will be, at that time: "An immense confidence in God's love."

If I look again at the question "Where do we go from here?" I have to say that the question can have no validity once there is no more time or space: there is no "where," in the sense that there is no space. We will enter eternity—which means entering a new life, a new way of living, a million times more real than this one, but real in another way. We understand as real what we can reach with our eyes and touch with our hands. But that will open in us the life of God, that will introduce us to the joy of God, the love of God, the security which is God himself. And to explain "where we are going," I should have to ask: "What is God?" He is the end of all exploration and travellings on earth. He is our new land, our new light, our new sun, our new warmth. I know that the eternal life to come in fullness is already given to me in baptism, on that very day. I have been baptized in the Father, the Son, and the Holy Spirit, which means that God is already in me from the very start of life. That will open the door, to make me discover the love of God for ever and ever. I will see with new eyes the glory of God, and discover with surprise how present he has been in my daily life, in the days of suffering as well as in the days of joy. Our life will be thanksgiving. We shall experience what it means to enter into the joy of the Lord. We are going from here to the Kingdom of God. Another surprise of heaven will be to discover the full meaning of the words "Kingdom of God"; for in God we shall find all the saints of the past who preceded us on the way to eternity—Mary and the apostles, the martyrs, the confessors, and all those we loved here on earth. It will be a communion.

I meditate very often upon the words of Saint Teresa: "In heaven everybody will smile at each other." Think of that. Go into the streets of any city, go to any airport, or any station, and look for a while at the faces of the people running through those places. Look at the faces. It is so rare to see a smile. Everybody is in a hurry. Everybody is busy with his own business. Nobody has time to really look at each other. We are millions who live in the same city, or the same street, but without any human communication.

Heaven will be a true community, a true family. This seems so paradoxical, but we will be no more isolated from each other. Holy Scripture tells us that God will be all in all at that final stage, and this will be our communitarian joy, to see each other with new eyes, to see what God did in each one of us, to see God shining through his creatures, to see the love and the beauty of God in every person we will meet eternally. This will be the end without end for which we are created. Remember the words of Saint Augustine: "Our heart, O Lord, is full of anguish until we find our rest and peace in you, only in you." Life after death, for a Christian, means rest and peace with God and in God, rest and peace with all our brothers known and unknown.

The question was: "Where do we go from here?" The answer is that death is a going into, not a going away from. We are going from time to eternity. We are going from death to life. We are going from passing suffering to everlasting joy. Praise the Lord.

The Council and Church Unity

Ecumenism in the Work of the Council

It is generally recognized that, unlike the Councils of Lyons or of Florence, the Second Vatican Council is not a council of reunion. That is to say that the effort of reconciliation is not the principal concern of the Council. But in no sense does it mean that the Council is not keenly aware of the need for mutual understanding.

It is not so much in the schema explicitly devoted to ecumenism that we find the best indication of this. Rather do we find it in the Council's basic drive toward renewal on every level.

Let us put some stress here on a few of the most important of the Council's indirect ecumenical contributions. These are of such a nature as to speed the greatly desired day when the visible unity of the Church will triumph over all obstacles, in full fidelity to the Lord's desire: "Father, that they may be one."

Vatican II's first ecumenical measure was the resumption of the work of Vatican I.

By its choice of the Church as its central theme, the Second Vatican Council placed itself in perfect continuity with Vatican I and provided the opportunity for clearing up certain misunderstandings and obscurities which followed on Vatican I. That Council, which so forcefully delineated the role of the primacy and of papal infallibility, was, of course, prevented from finishing its work by the War of 1870. This historical accident resulted in a one-sidedness in presentation. It was not possible to give attention to the schema which had been prepared on the nature of the Church, the role of the episcopacy, etc. As is commonly known, the Council Fathers had originally received for study a sizable schema, "On the Church of Christ," which treated the primacy of the Pope only in chapters 11 and 12, after having devoted the first ten chapters to consideration of the Church in general. The net result of all this was to give the impression that the Church was, for the future, to be thought of as absorbed in the person of her visible head, as if he had been detached and separated from the Church, and isolated from the episcopacy of the world. The whole of the Council's work in this second session will be an effort at completion, at harmonization, and at synthesis.

Although it will not be possible here to recapitulate all the discussions of the second session, so rich and variegated in the problems suggested, I would like to devote some time to several of the most important points which have marked this second phase, and whose ecumenical implications are unmistakable.

The people of God

The original schema *De Ecclesia*, which was submitted to the bishops for study, began with a chapter which undertook to define the mystery of the Church, then passed on immediately to a second chapter concerned with the hierarchy. As the one responsible for presenting the schema to the Coordinating Commission, I suggested a different order, and this was subsequently adopted by the Council. It consisted in having the first chapter followed, not by a consideration of the hierarchy, but by a second chapter which would treat the people of God. The study of the hierarchy's role was to be reserved for a third chapter.

The term "people of God," it should be noted, is not intended to signify the people constituted by the faithful as distinct from the hierarchy. It looks, rather, to the entirety of the members of the Church, pastors as well as faithful.

If it is true that the hierarchy, in certain respects, takes precedence over the faithful, since the faithful are brought by it to faith and to supernatural life, it remains no less true that pastors and faithful alike belong to the one people of God. The thought of God is directed to his people and its salvation; in regard to this end, the hierarchy is but a means. This is why our primary concern must be with the people of God as a totality before we proceed to a study of its various constituent parts and their mutual interrelationship.

Once this change of viewpoint is effected, a wholly new orientation is given to our reflections. What now first catches our eye is this community of those who are baptized, who are all made one by the same baptism. This impresses itself upon us, and makes its mark before there is an awareness of the various gifts and ministries.

This emphasis on the people of God—"a chosen race, a royal priesthood," in St. Peter's phrase (1 Pet. 2:9)—is an indication of how fully we have recovered our appreciation of this basic reality. We realize anew that the mission of giving Christ to the world falls on the entire Christian people, at every level, and no less imperatively for being diverse in manner.

It was in the light of all this that I felt I had the duty of drawing attention to the abiding nature of the charisms of the Holy Spirit within the people of God. Here is the substance of my address to the Council.

We often speak of the charisms of Christians, that is, the special gifts conferred on them by the Holy Spirit, as if we had here merely an accidental and marginal phenomenon in the life of the Church. It seems necessary then to show the importance of these charisms in the edification of the Mystical Body, for the hierarchical structure of the Church is something more than a mere administrative machine quite unrelated to the charismatic gifts which the Holy Ghost spreads throughout the Church. Pope Pius XII's encyclical, *Mystici Corporis*, has already dealt with this question, of course.

Charisms

The time which measures the march of the Church toward the Parousia of the Lord is the era of the Holy Spirit, by whose action the glorious Christ gathers together the people of God who are awaiting the Day of the Lord and purifies them, gives them life and leads them to the fullness of truth. The Holy Spirit, scripture tells us, is given to the Church in this world as first fruits and a pledge. That is why the Church is called "the dwelling of God in the Spirit" (Eph. 2:22).

The Holy Spirit is not given only to the pastors of the flock but to all Christians without exception: "Do you not know that you are a temple of God and that the Spirit of God dwells in you?" writes Saint Paul to the Corinthians (1 Cor. 3:16). In baptism, the sacrament of faith, all Christians receive the Holy Spirit. All are "living stones" which must play a part in raising a "spiritual edifice," "oikos pneumatikos" (1 Pet. 2:5). The whole Church, which is literally animated by the Spirit, stands founded on the apostles and also, as St. Paul says, on the prophets (Eph. 2:30). In the Church of the New Testament, God "has given to some to be apostles, to other prophets, or evangelists or else pastors and doctors . . ." (Eph. 4:11).

The Holy Spirit shows his presence in the Church by the abundance of his special gifts, called charisms in scripture. No doubt, at the time of St. Paul the Church witnessed charisms which were rather unusual and indeed astonishing, like the gift of tongues or the gift of healing. But we must not think that spiritual gifts consist exclusively or even principally in these rather spectacular manifestations.

St. Paul speaks as well of a gift of expounding the deepest religious truths (the charism of the word of wisdom) or of presenting the elementary teaching on Christ (the charism of the word of knowledge), or of the charism of faith, the charism of preaching, of exhortation or of consolation, or of service, of the charism of discernment of spirits, of giving help in need, of administering and ruling the churches, etc. (see Rom. 12 and 1 Cor. 12).

In the eyes of St. Paul, the Church of Christ is not an administrative organization. He sees it as a living whole made up of gifts, charisms, and services. The Spirit is given to all Christians; to all and to each he distributes his gifts and his charisms "which differ according to the grace which has been given us" (Rom. 12:6). In fact, "to each the manifestation of the Spirit is given for the common good" (1 Cor. 12:7), that is to say, "so that the Church may derive edification from it" (1 Cor. 14:12). Every Christian, educated or not, possesses even in his everyday life a spiritual gift proper to himself, but, as St. Paul says, to edify the Church.

When we hear the apostle affirm: "There are some whom God has raised up in the Church firstly as apostles, secondly as prophets, thirdly as doctors . . . Are all apostles? All prophets? All doctors? (1 Cor. 12:28), we realize that to speak of the Church thinking only of the apostles and their successors and forgetting the prophets and doctors, would mean neglecting an element of primary importance.

For what would our Church be without the charism of

the doctors, that is, the theologians? And what would become of it without the charism of the prophets, that is, those men who, under the inspiration of the Holy Spirit, persist in season and out of season and awaken a sleeping Church, lest the gospel in practice be neglected.

It was not only in the age of Thomas Aquinas or Francis of Assisi that the Church felt the need of the charisms of doctors, prophets, and other ministers. It needs them today, even in the most humdrum circumstances.

Let us speak of those charisms which arouse astonishment. Let us speak of the unsensational charisms. Do not all of us know those men and women raised up as it were by God himself on whom the Holy Spirit has bestowed gifts for catechizing, for evangelization, for Catholic Action in all its forms, for social and charitable action? Does not the experience of every day teach us that the action of the Holy Spirit is not finished in the Church?

It is obvious that without the intervention of the ecclesiastical authorities the action of charisms in the Church could produce anarchy. But on the other hand, without charisms the ecclesiastical ministry could produce poverty and sterility.

Let the pastors, both of single churches and the universal Church, have that kind of spiritual instinct which fosters the discovery of charisms, raises them up and develops them.

Let the pastors of the Church listen carefully and willingly to the laity and hold unceasingly an active dialogue with them. The laity have received their gifts of the Holy Ghost and often possess greater experience of the life of the modern world.

Let the pastors of the Church themselves desire better gifts (1 Cor. 12:31). All the faithful, even those endowed with the loftiest spiritual gifts, owe respect and obedience to their fathers in the faith. Correspondingly, attention and respect are owed to the gifts and impulses of the Holy Spirit who often inspires the action of simple and modest lay people. That is the reason why St. Paul warns all Christians, including the pastors: "Do not extinguish the Spirit. Do not despise the gifts of prophecy, but prove all things; hold fast to what is good" (1 Thess. 5:19-21). This mass of gifts, charisms, and services could not be put to work for the edification of the Church without the liberty of the children of God which the pastors, following the example of St. Paul, have a duty to protect and encourage.

Ministry

In the light of what has preceded, we see the sacerdotal, episcopal, and papal ministry as a means in the service of ecclesial community, rather than as an end. We can also see, in such a view of the Church, the manifold ecumenical implications.

The majority of the addresses at the Council stressed to how great an extent the ministry is *diakonia,* "service," and how great is the desire to do away with anything which makes it appear in the guise of power or domination.

The Church is divine and human at the same time. Since it is made up of men who bear the treasures of God in fragile vessels, it is constantly faced with the need of purification, of a perpetual return to its sources.

The symbolic expression of this return, already inherent in the Council, is something we all witnessed, when Paul VI went to Jerusalem with the sole intention of making a pilgrimage of prayer and penance. The initial intention did not go beyond that. The providential meeting with Patriarch Athenagoras was a further consequence which had not at first been foreseen.

The Church, it seems, is becoming increasingly conscious of the fact that all authority is service; it is a primacy of love: "Do you love me more than these?" (John 21:15). Authority is forgetfulness of self in the interests of furthering a coordination of energies and an authentic fraternal union.

It seems to me that the Church is moving toward the elimination of all that disfigures her true face. It seems too that the Holy Spirit is leading the Lord's ministers to realize more fully that they are "the servants of the servants of God," and to ponder the unforgettable scene of the washing of feet, by which the Master indicated to his disciples, for all ages to come, how he conceived the task and the function of the apostolic ministry, whatever its rank.

The First Vatican Council put the accent on the role of Peter and his successors. Vatican II, without turning its back on anything achieved thereby, is undertaking the task of mediating that achievement through a formulation which will avoid misunderstandings and bring out some complementary aspects of this truth. The role of Peter is indivisibly united to that of the Twelve. When we consider the place of the apostolic body of the Twelve, and of the episcopal body, its successor, we see how totally misleading it is to present the Church as an absolute monarchy. Peter and the Twelve together make but one. Peter is inconceivable without the Twelve and without the Church which is built on the apostles and the prophets. But the Twelve are likewise inconceivable without their head, who is the focal point of their unity and who strengthens his brethren in the faith.

Discussion of the episcopal collegiality opens the way to a better understanding and a more gracious reception of the Eastern Churches, which are so keenly sensitive to the irreplaceable role of the bishop, the head of the particular Church.

It is not fanciful to suggest that the discussion on collegiality was the providential preface to the meeting on the Mount of Olives of Paul VI and Athenagoras.

Liturgy

The best efforts of the first session of the Council were devoted to the schema on the liturgy. Approved by a virtually unanimous vote at the end of the second session, the constitution on the liturgy impresses one not only as the crowning achievement of a half-century's effort at liturgical renewal within the Church, but also—and it is to this that I would draw your attention— as a complex of significant efforts at *rapprochement* with our separated brethren, both Orthodox and Protestant.

I wish only to mention in passing:
—the provisions for the use of the vernacular which make possible a more living participation by the faithful in the liturgy of the mass;
—the provisions for a closer contact with the Word of God in the proclamation of Holy Scripture;
—the adaptation of the liturgy to the diversities among peoples by allowing for variations based on cultural differences;
—the provisions for concelebration of the mass and for communion under both species.

Ecumenism and Pope Paul VI

What is the mind of Pope Paul VI with regard to the orientation of the Council? It was very clearly brought to light in the address which he delivered on the occasion of his coronation: "We inherit with feeling the patrimony of our unforgettable predecessor, John XXIII, on this point. He, under the impulse of the Holy Spirit, brought into being immense hopes, which we consider it a duty and an honor not to disappoint.

"No more than he do we nourish illusions about the extent of the problem to be solved and the gravity of the obstacles to be surmounted. But—faithful to the great apostle whose name we have taken, 'Let us speak the truth in love' (Eph. 4:15)—we intend to seek support only in our weapons of truth and love, to continue the dialogue which has been begun, and, as far as possible, to further the work already undertaken."

To continue the dialogue

The significance of the Pope's declaration remains to be studied. "To continue the dialogue which has been begun, and to further the work already undertaken": there, certainly, we have the principal purpose of the Catholic ecumenical movement today.

A dialogue was begun, in a very special way, by the creation of the Secretariat for Unity. Undoubtedly, there was nothing new in the idea. Pope Leo XIII, on March 19th, 1895, had set up a "Pontifical Commission for Fostering the Reconciliation of Dissidents with the Church," but it had only a fleeting existence. The "Secretariat for the Promotion of Christian Unity," which was established by John XXIII on June 5th, 1960, responds better, it seems, to the hopes of the Church, which immediately perceived that, within the life and organization of the Catholic Church, the Secretariat is an official body which is in some way responsible for continuing the dialogue among all separated Christians.

This dialogue entered upon an important phase from the very start of the Second Vatican Council, to begin with, through the presence of forty non-Catholic "observers." After a week spent in getting acquainted with the machinery of the Council, the observers began to exchange views with a number of sympathetic bishops and, subsequently, with other bishops who were eager to acquire a more personal relationship with the representatives of people in their dioceses whom they knew only in very indirect fashion. This trend has not ceased to undergo impressive development. Conversations, receptions, occasional meetings are producing, by various means, a well-knit ecumenical fabric. And that, it seems to me, is in itself a permanent achievement of the Council.

But the Council Fathers themselves made it plain, by the overall tone of their addresses, that the dialogue had really gotten under way. Their insistence that the schemas give proof of a more explicitly ecumenical spirit is enough to establish that fact. And their frequent comments constituted a kind of doctrinal dialogue with participants who, although silent for the moment, later publicly expressed their thoughts and sentiments. The inevitable result of this is that the schemas will bear the mark of an ecumenical awareness and will stand, for generations to come, as the beginning of a trend which must not be reversed, as an ever-present symbol and as a summons to unceasing progress.

For this is going to be one of the dominant notes of the pontificate of Paul VI in regard to ecumenism: "to further the work already undertaken."

We must increase our mutual acquaintance. So many misunderstandings stem simply from the fact that separated Christians hardly know one another. Similarly, the causes of division, the intentions of past leaders, the various vicissitudes of these painful separations are too often known only in a very sketchy way.

We must also make more of certain forms of practical collaboration, notably in the social and humanitarian field: the problem of hunger in the world, sickness and disasters, birth and housing, illiteracy, redistribution of wealth, etc. In an era in which all men are conscious of the existence of extremely critical problems, it is essential that the disciples of Christ be able, *as Christians*, and without passing over or minimizing their differences, to get together and make common cause in every kind of mutual cooperation and assistance. We must increase our prayer, too, with a view to hastening the day of visible unity. The need for a "spiritual approach" to the problems of ecumenism could not be more clear. The Holy Spirit is at work in the movement toward unity which animates all Christ's disciples, as the Holy Office Instruction, *Ecclesia Catholica*, in 1949, made very clear. And all are familiar with the world-wide impact of the Church Unity Octave, the week of prayer which is especially set aside every January. We must accept the fact that unity is an ecclesial problem, which has to be squarely faced in its theological dimensions: on the level of the life of the Father and of the Son in the Holy Spirit.

Differences among Christians

"We nourish no illusions about the extent of the problems to be solved and the gravity of the obstacles to be surmounted," the Pope continued in his coronation address.

The problem is extensive indeed. All we have to do is look at the fact and figures. There are about nine hundred million Christians, half of whom are Roman Catholics. But, Christ, the "founder of Christianity," prayed on the eve of his death, "that they all may be one: as thou, Father, art in me, and I in thee" (John 14:21). Still more, these Christians stand face to face with two billion non-Christians, and to these they present, in division if not in discord, a religion which they loudly proclaim as the religion of charity: "By this all men will know that you are my disciples, if you have love for one another"

(John 13:35). This, to be sure, is merely the external dimension, but it may also be the greatest scandal of the entire situation.

The problem is also extensive in its interior dimension: there are the multiple difficulties inherent in the Christian "Churches" themselves which obstruct their reconciliation. Some of these difficulties are dogmatic in nature. Anyone who has perused the *Reports of the World Faith and Order Conferences* at Lausanne (1927), Edinburgh (1937), Lund (1952) and Montreal (1963) is forced to acknowledge the existence of a great many disagreements of dogmatic character even among the member Churches of the World Council of Churches. There are non-theological difficulties too. Today we recognize that social and cultural factors play no less decisive a role in obstructing reconciliation. Examples of these are the way in which the origin and present status of the separated "Churches" are presented in history courses; the gradual identification that can be observed between certain "Churches" and certain "nations"; the fact that the separated "Churches," in the course of centuries, make their differences more pronounced and become fixed in their estrangement; the influence of institutions and social structures, which often aggravate divergences and make them permanent; the psychological tendency to be content with the status quo, etc.

Renewal and ecumenism

For our own part, we wish to hasten God's hour by making continual efforts toward an ever-greater "renewal" in the Spirit and in the gospel. Our purpose in doing this is to put before all who are not Catholics a Church whose outward features, and whose doctrinal and dynamic poise, are as perfect as possible—that is, correspond as faithfully as possible to the desires of Our

Lord. The dogmatic difficulties are real ones, but it may well be that they are intensified by the theology which explains them, by the sort of argument which justifies them, by the way they are expressed in the organization and life of the Church. These, to be sure, are "accidental" considerations, but they have important consequences. There are, unquestionably, component factors in the unity of the Church which cannot be compromised; but it is not inconceivable that, in the name of this very unity, we are imposing on "others"—under pain of remaining outside the Catholic Church— theories, forms of spirituality, behavioral norms, in short, an entire way of life and a set of requirements which are simply not essential to Catholic unity.

By accomplishing this renewal in themselves, Catholics will simply be responding to one of the purposes of the Second Vatican Council. We all remember Pope John's intentions in summoning it. What we must strive to achieve, he said, is a work of adaptation— *aggiornamento*—a spiritual awakening, a newness of life throughout the Church which will enable her to appear in all her beauty. Then, he went on, once we have accomplished this arduous task, by eliminating everything that, on the human plane, could slow down our progress, we will present the Church in the fullness of her splendor, *sine macula et sine ruga.* Thus, from one of the major goals of the Second Vatican Council, we are given an insight into its specifically "ecumenical" nature. And this extremely solemn appeal of Pope and Council is addressed to the entire Christian community. But we must recognize that it is not in books or in archives that separated Christians hope to find this spiritual renewal, this candor, this doctrinal and dynamic poise. Nor is it even in the schemas of Vatican II. They hope to find them, before all else, in the community of the faithful, as it exists and as it thinks and prays and acts. It is through

107

the body of Catholics as a whole and through each individual Catholic, through their spirituality, their ideas, their attitudes, that Protestants and Orthodox come into contact with Catholicism. It is the entire body of Catholics and each individual Catholic who trace out, by all that they are and all that they do, the characteristic features of the Church as seen by the separated brethren. To put it briefly, just as we judge Lutheranism on the basis of the image Lutherans present, and not merely on the basis of professions of faith, so too do Protestants judge Catholicism in the light of the image presented by the members of the Catholic community. During a period of ecumenism, every Catholic must assume an awesome responsibility, for he stands for the whole Church.

With regard to the results of ecumenism—if, indeed, a human estimate is of any value—we must not "nourish illusions," as if final union were scheduled for tomorrow. "First an approach, then a reconciliation, and finally perfect reunion" is how Pope John expressed it. We are still at the stage of "approach," brightened by several reconciliations. The collective ecumenical effort of the Catholic Church is of relatively recent origin; it is developing by leaps and bounds, but it is premature to attempt to estimate in human terms what the future holds in store. A separation which has endured for many centuries, particularly where religious institutions are involved, leaves deep wounds which cannot be expected to heal rapidly. Mutual understanding among the Churches is going to demand a great many adaptations. These, beyond any question, will transform both men and organizations, but it will be at a slow and measured pace, a pace which will sometimes be uncertain. If it is extremely difficult to arouse the entire Christian people to a consciousness of being "in state of mission," it is going to be every bit as arduous to involve the entire Church in an "ecumenical age."

Our task is to sow the seed; others, perhaps, will reap the harvest; the gospel adage will be found no less true today than ever. It is for each one of us, then, to ponder the task required of him and to respond according to the mission the Lord entrusts to him: the one who presides over the community must give it its orientation; the one who has the opportunity for prayer must unite his prayer to the Lord's prayer for unity (John 17); the one who is able to study must communicate the fruits of his research; the one who suffers must offer to the cause of unity this participation in the Passion of the Savior. And the Lord, whose generosity is boundless, will see to successful completion the work whose first steps he has inspired and whose first fruits he has brought to maturity.

Metholology of ecumenism

If, at the end of this rapid sketch of the Council and of the Pope's thought, considered from an ecumenical standpoint, someone were to ask me to outline the basic conditions for tomorrow's ecumenical dialogue, I would say that they could be reduced to the following principles.

1. Our ecumenism must be supernatural. There has been talk of the ecumenism of the smile. Such ecumenism is a beginning, but it is a good way still from Christian ecumenism. A simple, vaguely defined desire for contact is far from sufficient, for this kind of desire can just as easily be motivated by the wish to appear broad-minded, or generous, or gracious; it can also be motivated by the desire to unite against the great common enemy, atheistic communism, or by the intention of furthering a collective social effort. But an ecumenism which is satisfied with such motivations is wholly lacking in roots.

Our ecumenism must proceed from the very heart of God, who left to his disciples as a sacred testament the order to unite, to "be one that the world might believe that Jesus is the ambassador of God" (John 14:23). Our concern here is God's glory and the salvation of the world. And we must never allow human prudence to take precedence over fidelity to the fundamental realities.

A supernatural ecumenism will spring from prayer, a prayer which is mutual in intention at least, a prayer which is persevering, heartfelt, impatient with all the impatient love of God. We cannot conclude this prayer, whose unmatched model remains the Our Father, without the words: *"forgive us our trespasses as we forgive."* Paul VI's plea for mutual forgiveness, voiced at the opening of the second session of the Council, has its roots in the underlying logic of our Christian faith.

We must not shy away from the admission that the work of God has been hindered by the weight of our sins. Our acknowledgment of this fact must be both personal and collective. How great is the difficulty we encounter in overcoming our own sinfulness, and yet we act as if we were hypnotized by the faults committed by others in our regard. What we all need is an ever more vivid awareness of our own faults. This is absolutely essential for effective action toward mutual understanding.

Even when thus assured of its supernatural authenticity, ecumenism must respect certain other criteria which are more intimately related to what I might call the methodology of mutual understanding.

2. *We must not approach our doctrinal differences in the abstract, but must go back to the historical situation which brought them about.* It was not Mary that Luther was combating; it was certain abuses in Mariology. It

was not the idea of the episcopacy or the idea of the papacy which were first attacked; it was their realization in men of flesh and blood, men of a specific time and a specific environment who were inevitably influenced by that time and environment. We must have the ability to recognize the object of protest if we are ever going to appreciate the character of the reaction which it evoked and the germ of truth which animated it. Once we have recovered our historical perspective, a great many theses which have been petrified by the process of abstraction will profit from a suppleness and feeling for nuance which can reconcile in synthesis factors which are not contradictory but complementary.

This has been put very well by Hans Küng in *The Council, Reform and Reunion:* "To whatever extent the Protestant protest is justified, it is the Catholic Church herself, against whom the protest is made, who must take it up . . ."

3. *We must not confuse unity and uniformity.* The Church of Christ is one. But its unity dwells in the depths of mystery. It does not dispense with diversity of gifts and charisms any more than it dispenses with the diversity of languages and cultures.

It is of crucial importance for us to appreciate the fact that the Church, which is independent of all cultures, is nonetheless open to every culture. In their regard, the Church is transcendent—since she is not of this world; and yet, she is incarnate in each culture—like the leaven in the dough which can never be separated from it.

Respect for this unity in diversity is particularly evident in the Church's refusal to identify herself with the Latin Church. And we see it in very positive fashion in her openness to the Oriental tradition.

4. *If the dialogue is to be fruitful, it must avoid the*

characteristics of debate. A well-known controversialist remarked one day: "Every time I win an argument, I lose a soul." The debate approach, taken by itself, fosters opposition and emphasizes differences. "Every error," it has been said, "is nothing but the abuse of some truth." We must seek this germ of truth, this aspect of the real which is obscured by the opposite thesis. Only after we have found it and fully accepted it can we propose a complementary truth which will help us to discover the truth in all its integrity.

5. *In order to meet one another in a spirit of unity, we must each strive to discover mutually complementary factors which have not been experienced with the same intensity.* Shortly after the meeting of Paul and Athenagoras in Jerusalem, an Orthodox theologian offered this description of the road ahead: "We can only hope that future ecumenical measures of the two Churches"—he was speaking of the Church of Rome and of Constantinople—"will be marked by a creative fidelity which will enable each Church gradually to discover the other, so to speak, within her very self, as her 'other half' which, since the separation, has been insufficiently actualized and is today reacquired by the generous gift of God." In order to make this mutual discovery, we must get our bearings in the living experience of the Church, antecedently to any theological formulation.

6. *Finally—and this is of capital importance—our quest for the truth and our communion in love must be one thing.* We must always come back to St. Paul's words to the Ephesians: *Aletheuontes in agape.* 'Let us speak the truth in love" (Eph. 4:15). Duty toward truth, duty toward love: We need both. Charity simply cannot dispense with respect for the truth.

There is nothing more dangerous in such matters than

the achievement of peace by means of compromise, to the detriment of divine truth. Our charity would indeed be poor and unenlightened if we were to minimize our differences and seek to reduce God's truth to the dimensions of a newborn human wisdom.

Scripture tells us that we must walk before God "in truth and with a perfect heart" (cf. Isaiah 38:3). Truth first, in order to guide our love: this is the Savior's law. The truth must be loved above all things and must be served first. Man's need for truth is like a plant's need for the sun: he can only find fulfillment in a climate where everything bears its proper name, where every "Yes" is "Yes," and every "No" means "No." This uncompromising honesty toward the truth, however great or slight, is the necessary condition for all fruitful and lasting action. This love of the truth, faithfully sought and loved for its own sake, as a pure reflection of the face of God, can alone protect us or liberate us from all the "powerful illusions" of which St. Paul speaks (2 Thess. 2:11). Christ had nothing else in mind when he gave men a message that is valid for all ages: "The truth will set you free" (John 8:32).

But if charity cannot be separated from the search for the truth, truth itself is only fully true when it is completely penetrated by love.

At the end of a lecture on ecumenism, Pastor Marc Boegner magnificently expressed this immanence of truth in love. His words will serve as my own conclusion.

"There is no Christian truth, no truth of God, no truth of the Lord Jesus Christ, where there is no love. Christian truth communicated without love is not truth. Professor Jean Bosc has some splendid words on this subject. I ask your permission to read them: 'Christian truth is no longer itself when it is not indivisibly bound up with charity. And in a like manner, charity is charity only in truth.' The reason for this is simply that the truth of God

113

is the truth of the love which is his very being. God is love. And his love is the revelation and the manifestation of *his* truth. The abstract truth of charity, like an abstract love of truth, cannot be anything but a caricature.

" 'Only love matters,' said the dying St. Therese of Lisieux, so many of whose words find echoes in the hearts of all Christians, whatever their confession. 'Only love matters' because love bears within itself the essential truth of God.

"Nothing is going to be accomplished for the cause of Church unity by the World Council of Churches or the Second Vatican Council if theologians stop at theological discussions and if they do not begin by begging the grace of love and of mediation which springs from a true fraternal charity. We are not concerned with sentimentalism. We are concerned with taking part in a great drama, in the wonderful adventure of God who is love and who is calling us by his love alone, a love which went to the very limit of Calvary's cross. He calls us to become one in the love with which we are loved, to become one in him who has ever loved us first, to become one in him to whom we must offer the poor response of our own love by first loving one another—we who profess, Catholics or Protestants, to be his disciples. Oh, that we might learn how to put aside all the weapons of flesh and blood, all the distrust, the suspicion, the hostility, the polemics. Let us put on the armor of soldiers of the light, as St. Paul exhorted us (Rom. 13:12). Or, rather, let us ask the grace of being clothed in it by him who alone can do so. And thus let us attain, in one another's regard, to that candor which is essential if we truly desire to work together in this immense task and which will make it possible for the sacerdotal prayer to be heard. Pere Charles de Foucauld once used these words with which you are probably all familiar: 'Jesus is master of the impossible.' Yes, we are face to face with the impossible;

yes, the doctrinal barriers appear and indeed are, for the moment, insurmountable from the human point of view; but Christ himself has told us that 'what is impossible with man is possible with God' (Luke 18:27). It is possible with God when his children give themselves over completely to the action of grace and thus become the artisans of that possibility."*

*From the lecture "Le conseil oecuménique des eglises a l'approche du Concile du Vatican," delivered by Pastor Marc Boegner in Strasbourg, France, on November 13, 1961, at a conference in the annual series "Les humanités chrétiennes," and published in *L'Eglise en dialogue* [Paris: Editions du centurion, 1962], pp. 101-102.

Toward Tomorrow's Church

A few months ago when I arrived at the airport in London, Canada, a journalist asked to interview me. He said, "I don't ask you for a long interview; I have just one question. Is the Church today in a state of evolution or a state of revolution?" I had just a second of time to invoke the Holy Spirit—I believe strongly in the Holy Spirit's role at just the right moment—and I said, "Well, sir, 'revolution' is too strong and 'evolution' is too weak."

It might be good to consider a moment why neither word is quite right. "Revolution" is not the correct term because, when you speak about the Church of God, there will never be the sort of break with the past that revolution brings. You can speak about the French Revolution, meaning a break with history, or the Russian Revolution, meaning a break with Czarism. But you should never speak about a revolution in the Church because the Church is rooted in continuity with the past.

Not only Christ and his apostles twenty centuries ago make up the Church's past; for there is a continuity from the beginning of the old covenant, a fidelity of God, so the Church is always in tradition in that sense. I find such strength when, in the moments before communion, during the eucharist, I pray that simple and so profound prayer, "Lord, don't look at my sins but look at the faith of your Church." I believe not only with my own poor personal faith, but with the faith of Abraham, of the Patriarchs, of the Prophets, with the faith of Mary, with the faith of the Apostles—Peter, Paul, the Twelve—with the faith of the confessors, the saints, the mystics. All that continuity is mine. It is a very strong continuity, so we can never use the word "revolution" when speaking of change in the Church.

Not evolution

On the other hand, the word "evolution" is too weak. We are not in the middle of a smooth development like a seed becoming a tree, an acorn becoming an oak, or a child becoming an adult. We are living in something more profound. It is difficult to find the exact word. I should say it is more a mystery of renovation in depth. Renovation like a seed in the ground preparing for the spring-time while it is still winter. We are in between: no longer winter, not yet spring. Because the renovation in depth is going on so profoundly, this is the grace we are living today.

In some aspects it is a mystery like Good Friday: a certain Church is dying, a new Church is coming out. It is the same Church but with a sort of renewed image, as if we are shining lights on some aspects of the Church which we did not illuminate enough in the past. And, of course, once we shine the full light on some points, we cast others into shadow. This does not mean that those other points cease to exist, but rather they receive new proportions, new perspectives, new orientation.

To situate ourselves as a pilgrim Church on the road, we must first inquire from where we are coming and then ask where we are going. These are the two questions I wish to consider here.

From where are we coming? The decade of the sixties was dominated by Vatican II: first the preparation, then the event, then the implementation—the slow and difficult implementation—of the Council. The process is still not finished. But the Council is the main point we see when we look at the immediate past.

Now many are saying today that the cause of all our trouble is Vatican II. I disagree. I think when Vatican II started, the Holy Spirit gave a ray of light and warmth to his church. It was just like the sun coming out and shining on a mountain snowcap. As the snow and ice melted, water soon began to run down, forming torrents, moving stones, and engulfing trees until the waters find a channel and move slowly to the sea.

The reason for the trouble of today is not that Vatican II started the process of renovation, but that for so long the Church remained in a sort of immobility. The previous Council, Vatican I, took place nearly a century ago. The process of continuous adaptation was not at work. Of course we had all sorts of changing to do. For example the liturgy had been unchanged for four centuries. The legacy of immobility is one of the reasons for today's ferment.

Pope John opened Vatican II by saying he hoped it would be a "new Pentecost." I believe the decade we are just beginning will bear out his wish.

Structural renewal

Vatican II concentrated on one topic: the renewal of the Church. And because Church renewal was the focus, the decade of 1960-1970 shone its full light on the structural, institutional side of the Church. This was a time for thinking through all sorts of needed adaptations in the visible structure.

Of course, there is always a tension between the Church as an institution and the Church as an invisible mystery of God. Never may we separate the two. We cannot separate the visible Church and the invisible, pneumatic, charismatic Church. But there is always in the unity of the one Church a sort of tension between the visible and the invisible, between body and soul.

Advocates of both aspects need mutual understanding. And from time to time, the Holy Spirit is there to remind us all that priority must be given to the spirit, to the soul.

Today we are living out the process begun in Vatican II, a Council that focused on the institutional aspect of the Church. That process is continuing: it is not finished. We need to put in action on every level what is often only in the planning stage. At the parish level, we see parish councils joining with the priest in his apostolic field, just as they join him when he celebrates mass. Consider how, in the past, the priest was alone, his back turned to the people, saying mass in Latin, without real communication. But now we are around him, celebrating with him. It is a unity, a communion in prayer to the Lord. Yet we are not fully a communion, either toward God or toward the world; we don't as yet fully reflect in our communion the light and warmth of God. We are building, but we are in the early stages.

The same is true for priests' councils. Instead of keeping priests and bishops aloof from one another, we feel the need to bring them together for dialogue and for a level of sharing that is deeper than just dialogue. It must be a communion, a unity between priests and bishops in such a way that it is the presbyterium as such which does the priestly work.

Priesthood means the priesthood of Christ, so that we are all in communion with Christ. Now, if we try to make all the juridical distinctions about that—what exactly is the right of a priest, exactly the right of a bishop, and so on—the attempt is bound to fail. Granted we need some minimal juridical expressions, but we at all times must be aware that we are dealing with a mystery of communion.

For instance, when I concelebrate mass with twenty other priests around me and I pronounce the words of the consecration, the consecration is there. But the twenty priests around me are pronouncing the same words and they also are consecrating. If someone asks what is my part or what is their part, I can only answer that we are in a mystery of communion.

At another level of collectivity, the synod of bishops is a working example of what collegiality could be. Here collegiality is a most appropriate term, because Christ founded his Church on Peter and the Twelve together. The Twelve with Peter; under Peter, but with Peter. In the synod of bishops we have one instrument for this collegiality. The work is far from being finished. The synod is a first step toward the full communion we must have if we are to more fully realize the mystery of God. We must be aware at all times that we are not just constructing juridical organizations and councils, for we are trying to find on different levels that communion in the Spirit of God: laity with priests, priests with bishops, bishops with Pope. We are going toward it, but we are not yet at the final stage.

There is always a danger when we think about the Church in human terms. Of course, the Church is a visible body since its members are visible bodies and we need a certain minimum of laws. But we do not need a maximum of laws. I am always very afraid when something like a Lex Fundmentalis comes out. It is good to see that a vast majority of the bishops rejected it. There is always such a danger when one attempts to enunciate in human terms the mystery of God in the Church, the communion with the Father, Son, and Holy Spirit. This mysterious communion is the depth of the meaning when you say "Church." At once you feel how inadequate human words can be.

The Church is not a democracy. The reality is much deeper than that. We are the People of God; but, when you speak in human terms of the "people," you tend to think of "people" in opposition to "government." Now when we speak about the People of God in the Church, we mean all the baptized children of God—Pope, bishops, and laity. Once we stress that truth about the People of God, we can see that we are living in deep communion with each other; we are not a people set in opposition to their leaders.

Unity and plurality

The same is true when we use the words "plurality," "diversity," and "unity." The interrelation of these has to be seen in a new light of the mystery of God. When I speak about unity and plurality, about the one unique Church and, at the same time, a communion of Churches, my language reflects the mystery of unity and plurality of the Trinity itself. God is one and God is one in three persons. One and three. If you put that in mathematical terms, you are lost because the depth of the unity is so profound. There is unity in that plurality; and there is plurality in that unity. This is the sort of unity we find in the plurality of the Churches: a unity, but not necessarily a uniformity. When St. Paul speaks about the local Churches, the Churches of Jerusalem and Ephesus and Rome, he does not use the word "the Church"; he always uses the term, "The Church of God" (note the singular) "which is in Ephesus," or "the Church of God which is in Rome."

We are part of the same Church but in a diversity of time and space. In the same way, I say that Christ is totally present in one host, yet he is totally there in the multiplicity as well. We must always clarify our notions

121

so as to respect the mystery of God.

The institutional process must continue, for we are only at the beginning. However, at every step, the process must be allowed to develop in the light of the mystery of God. We must carry on that sort of work all the time, not with human lights, but in the light of the Spirit of God who leads all Christians at every level to communion.

Even there I use a human word. "Level" is a bad word because there are no levels. We are one and the same. There is not a division of levels into heart and feet and hands. There is no question of speaking about powers to do that. We are in complementarity; all those charisms are working together. Of course, the functions are diverse. Everybody is not doing the same thing. But their essential unity depends on their common starting point—baptism.

Charismatic renewal

If we know where we are coming from, we can ask where we are going. From here to where? Projecting the future on the basis of the present, I would say that we are entering a new evangelical time and a new charismatic time for the Church of God.

It is difficult to make a distinction between evangelical and charismatic. There is a distinction between the Spirit of Christ and Christ himself, but at the same time there is such a unity that I will not divide the subject. In the same way, Christ is working today through the Holy Spirit for the evangelical renewal, the Pentecostal renewal, of his Church. I think what is coming and what is badly needed is a renewal of spirituality among the Christians of today. When I say "spirituality," I use an abstract word, but spirituality means, "Holy Spirit at work." The Holy Spirit is working profoundly to renew his Church from the inside. Something has been done and will continue to be done to renew the visible body; but at the same time we are experiencing a less evident renewal of the invisible side, the Pentecostal side, of the Church.

This is not to say that in the earlier decade we were only open to institutional renewal. But these institutional reforms have had the most importance in the public eye because it is always easiest to appreciate what is visible to everyone. But I suggest the time has come to appreciate the more profound element in renewal. If you wish to renew an automobile, of course you must discuss gears and brakes and air conditioning and windows. But even the most wonderful car is useless without that little tiny thing called a key. And even with the perfect key, the car is still useless without gasoline.

In Church of today, our key is contact with Christ. We must renew that contact, renew our understanding of who Christ is. The fuel that supplies energy is the activity of the Holy Spirit, who stirs up faith and hope and charity in the soul of each of us. Real Church renewal happens in each of us; for we, after all, are the Church. We are so accustomed to speak about the Church as something outside us, forgetting that we are the Church, all of us together.

So if now the accent is on that invisible spiritual part of the Church, then every family is in a way a little Church, because, when you have communion, you have the beginning of a Church. Even Vatican II in the Dogmatic Constitution on the Church used the word to speak about the family. "The little domestic Church," it said. The first image of a communion of love is there in the love between wife and husband. There you have the Church in its elements; and the Church at large, like a human body, will only be the sum of the little images, the cells.

So our challenge today is to give to Jesus Christ the central place in our lives. Will we Christians really be

123

what our name signifies: one with Christ? Will we open ourselves to be possessed by him so we can honestly say, "I am not living; it is Christ living in me, loving in me, speaking through me, smiling through me, going and coming through me?" We cannot have a eucharist without some bread and wine; we cannot have a baptism without water. Well, so too, Christ cannot live his life today in this world of ours without our mouth, without our eyes, without our going and coming, without our heart. For he wishes to love through our heart. When we love, he loves through us. This is Christianity.

Making Christ visible

Such is Jesus' challenge to his Church, the question he is putting to each of us today more than ever. It is the same question he put to his apostles on the roads of Palestine when he turned to them with the query, "Who do you say I am?" This is the vital question because all depends on the answer we give it. And the world will not just accept the answer on the lips. It will also ask, "How do you translate your faith into acts of Christianity? Can I see Christ in you?" Scripture tells us about a little group of people who came to the apostle Philip and said to him, "We wish to see Jesus." That is a permanent wish. All the unbelievers, all the non-Christians are just looking at us, wishing to see Jesus in us.

Here, I think, is the credibility gap between the new and the older generations. Nobody reproaches us because we are Christians. For everybody admires the gospel. But the young do not see Christ in the Christians. We can only create that new generation of Christians if we make something personal of our meeting with Christ.

This is the place where we have lost some credibility. In the past, many Christians were simply "sociological" Christians—men and women who were Christians because the society was Christian. In many countries, everybody was Christian because everyone shared the same climate of faith. The sons followed their fathers and grandfathers into the Church.

This climate of faith—including all the exterior helps that supported the faith—has now disappeared. We now make our decison for Christ by ourselves. Christ must be the biggest decision in our life. The meaning, the essence, the value of my life, of my sufferings, of my joys, of time and eternity—all that is Christ. So there is the issue.

A priest in my diocese once told me, "When I was in seminary, I learned an answer to every question you could imagine. Unhappily, nobody asked me those questions." Today we know the question: Christ is *the* question.

Recently a troubled priest came to me and said, "I wish to ask you just one question. What's the meaning of Christ for you personally? I don't want to discuss anything else. Just that."

So I spoke out of the depth of my heart. I told him that Christ was for me the meaning of life, the light of life, that his words in the gospel were creating life, were creating joy, were creating peace, that Christ was meant as hope and joy and peace through every suffering you can imagine, but that he was the permanent joy, the expression, the incarnation of love of God for mankind and for me. This is the question they will put to you directly, too.

I think that today we are discovering more and more the genuine humanity of Christ. Of course, Christ is at the same time fully human and fully divine. We must resist the mental temptation to think about Christ as fifty-fifty: partially human, partially divine. He is completely human and completely divine. We must also resist the notion that he is human in spite of his divinity. To the contrary, he is human because of his divinity. His humanity is so human that it is transcendentally human. He is human in a unique way because he is the unique Son of God.

You can almost feel that Christ, only Christ, is completely human. He does not condense in himself all the qualities of all men. No, he is completely human in such a way that he makes you feel that you are not human enough yourself.

Two or three times I have met genuine saints—people who have been possessed by Christ—and I have always been struck by the humanity of such people. They were so human that we are almost barbarians in comparison. Theirs is the Christ we have to discover. We must also discover him as a person who grows from a child among children to a man among men, not just *as if* he were human but as a natural consequence of his full humanity.

Many of us have a notion that John's baptism of Jesus—accompanied by a voice from heaven saying "This is my beloved Son, listen to him"—was a sort of a drama acted for other people. Not so, because this baptism had a meaning for Christ himself. When the battle and the agony came, Jesus was really a man in battle with the will of God, saying, "Must I go so far and so deep? Must I accept all the suffering and live through abandonment by God on behalf of all the brethren?" He assumed all the suffering for all of us, even the unrecognized but profound abandonment by those who do not know God. And he entered into it with all his humanity. This is what we have to discover.

Mary

Once we really believe in Christ's full humanity, see that we could encounter him on the street, open up to him, form a friendship with him, we can feel the role of his mother. Mary did not just give birth to him and follow

126

him. All that Christ was, humanly speaking, he received from his mother. I do not think we see this clearly enough after Vatican II. Some ambiguity was created, as if we drew too much light away from our Blessed Lady in trying to light up the underemphasized elements of the faith. Of course the light must always shine most brightly on Christ. But we cannot separate Christ and his mother.

Recently, I asked the famous theologian Karl Rahner why today there is some sort of aloofness toward our Blessed Lady. His answer was very striking. He said: "I think so many Christians of today have made Christianity into an ideology, a *Weltanschauung,* a vision of the mind, an abstraction." And then he added, "Abstractions don't need a mother."

The Spirit today

Christ is not an abstraction. He is the soul of the Church. He is the reality, the personality, the meaning of the Church. He is present today in his Church, present through his Spirit.

Thus, renewal of the Church means that we must make a new discovery of the Holy Spirit in today's Church. We have not paid sufficient attention to that part of Jesus' last testament when he said to his apostles, "I still have many things to say to you, but they would be too much for you now." His words apply now to each of us. Jesus has much to say to you, but it would be too difficult to hear it all now, so tomorrow he may well say something unexpected. He must reveal his love for you and what he is expecting from you. Jesus said, "You cannot bear it now. But, when the Spirit of truth comes, he will lead you to the complete truth. He will not be speaking from himself but will say only what he has learned, and he will tell you of the things to come. He will glorify me since all he tells you will be taken from what is mine."

This is our future: to make that sort of discovery of what the Holy Spirit means here and now. The Holy Spirit takes the words of Christ in the gospel and makes them actual for us now. This is what Jesus meant when he said, "My words are not just light for the spirit. My words are Spirit and life." As the scripture says, "You will not even understand God if you don't love." To understand God, we must open our souls and minds to the creative power of his word. His words bring meaning into daily life.

I know Christians who select a single line from the gospel each week and then discuss how they lived it, how they translated God's word into action. When we do this, we experience the gospel in a new way, as if we had never heard the words before. One day, a word will be spoken to you and it will change your life. This is the doing of the Holy Spirit.

This has happened to nearly every saint. One day a fellow called Francis of Assisi read a line of scripture and his life became an illustration of that single word. The same can be true for us. Just open the gospel and ask the Holy Spirit to put his light for you on the word in front of you. Jesus not only spoke twenty centuries ago; he is speaking now. Today.

When the famous theologian Karl Barth was the minister of a church in Switzerland, someone once asked him the secret of his carefully prepared homilies. He replied, "I take the gospel in one hand and the morning newspaper in the other, and I try to see what the light of the gospel is telling me about the deeds of the day." The Spirit, through the gospel, enters into dialogue with the present, and thus prepares the Church so he can lead it into the future.

Once we gain this confidence in the continuity guaranteed by the presence of the Holy Spirit, we can accept relativity, changes, and whatever else history will teach us. There are so many things that we may tend to see as absolutes revealed by God but which are really just conditioned by time. For example, suppose that Peter had remained in that oriental city Antioch, instead of going to live in Rome. The essence of the papal primacy would have remained unchanged. However, the way of exercising the primacy would have been completely different. The style would have been oriental, not Roman: all the influences of history would have been different.

What is essential to the Church is the continuity with the core elements Christ meant his Church to have. The Spirit guarantees this continuity, even as he creates in each era something that is both old and new.

We can always see new movements of the Spirit coming along. I think the Spirit is at work in a very special way in the charismatic renewal. I see the Spirit in other movements, such as the Marriage Encounter and the Focolare Movement. We must be ready to accept the fullness of his message for the Church today and of tomorrow. This work of the Holy Spirit will make the pilgrim Church of tomorrow more and more the Church of Christ and his Spirit. I can say without any hesitation that the institutional side of the Church will continue to be changed from within.

Church unity

The Holy Spirit will also enliven all the Christian Churches if we open ourselves to that new understanding of Christ and the Spirit. Of course, we ought to continue the dialogue among the Christian Churches to find that visible unity which was really in the heart and the wish of Christ. We must continue that dialogue on every level: institutional, theological, in formal and informal meetings. These efforts have been fruitful, and should be continued.

But the final solution will not come by high-level

dialogue among the Churches. It will finally come by searching together to be united with the same Christ, the same Spirit. It will be like receiving Communion. At the eucharist I receive the body and blood of Christ, not to transform Christ in me but to be transformed in him. So if all the Christian Churches are seeking Jesus Christ and letting Christ unite through himself, then unity will indeed come.

I feel that the Holy Spirit is working to bring about this unity. I can sense it in the remarks of leaders of other Christian Churches. As my good friend Archbishop Ramsey said recently: "Far and wide we have come to realize what the ecumenical task really is. It doesn't mean asking, 'How may we unite our Churches as they are now?' It means asking, 'How may our Churches become more Christ-like, more obedient to Christ's purpose for them?' "

The Orthodox theologian Meyendorff wrote these very profound words: "Christianity has suffered enough because it identified itself with power, with the state, with money, with the establishment. Many of us rightly want to disengage it from these embarrassing areas; but in order to win its true freedom, the Church must become itself again, not simply change camps, but become itself again." The meaning of that is becoming Christ again. There we have the future of ecumenism.

Often I am asked, "Will we see some sort of Vatican III?" I do not know. I am not a prophet, but I do have dreams. My dream is that one day we should see some sort of Jerusalem II. All Christians would come back to the Cenacle of Jerusalem for that new Pentecost. I dream that we shall come together to find Christ where he started and to discover Christianity with new eyes in the fullness of the Spirit of Pentecost.

The agenda for such a meeting should be a rediscovery in depth of the Holy Spirit, the Spirit of Jesus bringing us together. The Orientals reproach us Occidentals because we understress the role of the Holy Spirit. I think many objections would disappear if we put that squarely in front of us as our principal agendum: The Holy Spirit given to the People of God. I think the Churches of the Reform would readily accept such a dialogue focused on the Spirit of God who brings us together.

What will tomorrow be like? I do not know. One thing is important as we move forward. Be open for the personal understanding, the discovery of Christ in your life, for the discovery of the Spirit of Christ. Let him do his work in you. In his name I promise you joy, peace, hope, and happiness.